Reflections on the Sacrificial Death of Jesus Christ

Reflections on the Sacrificial Death of Jesus Christ

Daily Readings for Lent

Jason R. Tatlock

CASCADE *Books* · Eugene, Oregon

REFLECTIONS ON THE SACRIFICIAL DEATH OF JESUS CHRIST
Daily Readings for Lent

Cascade Books
An Imprint of Wipf and Stock Publishers
199 W. 8th Ave., Suite 3
Eugene, OR 97401

www.wipfandstock.com

PAPERBACK ISBN: 978-1-5326-9032-7
HARDCOVER ISBN: 978-1-5326-9033-4
EBOOK ISBN: 978-1-5326-9034-1

Cataloguing-in-Publication data:

Names: Tatlock, Jason., author.

Title: Reflections on the sacrificial death of Jesus Christ : daily readings for Lent / Jason Tatlock.

Description: Eugene, OR: Cascade Books, 2019. | Includes bibliographical references.

Identifiers: ISBN 978-1-5326-9032-7 (paperback). | ISBN 978-1-5326-9033-4 (hardcover). | ISBN 978-1-5326-9034-1 (ebook).

Subjects: LCSH: Lent—Prayers and devotion—English. | Church year meditations. | Devotional literature.

Classification: BX2170 L4 T21 2019 (print). | BX2170 (ebook).

Manufactured in the U.S.A.   SEPTEMBER 25, 2019

Contents

Preface

I specialize in the study of human sacrifice. I am trained in the history, languages, geography, and religions of the ancient Near East with a focus on ancient Israel and surrounding areas. My scholarship centers upon human rights and killing rites. A strange combination to be sure. I have published on the use of the Bible at the United Nations, for instance, but also on a variety of sacrificial issues, ranging from the ancient Mediterranean sphere to modern India. I am in the processing of finalizing an academic book on human sacrifice in the ancient world with Eisenbrauns publishers. The book surveys Greek, Roman, Punic, and Near Eastern material from prehistory into the Roman era and beyond, and it interacts with numerous scholarly publications. The work you are about to read is completely different. *Reflections* is a devotional study based almost entirely upon my analysis of the New Testament in the light of the Hebrew Bible (or Old Testament). It was mainly written in the winter of 2015–2016 when I felt compelled to provide a series of daily reflective readings on Jesus' sacrificial crucifixion. As an academic who mainly writes for and works in non-confessional contexts, preparing *Reflections* was challenging at times. Scholars do not typically write about their personal beliefs, much less their faith struggles. I share both. Perhaps you will be able to identify with some of what I have written. I hope that you will be inspired. I desire that you will come to a deeper appreciation for the complex representation of Jesus' death as a human sacrifice by spending the days of Lent with me. Of course, you can read this work at any time of the year.

Acknowledgments

Several individuals have participated in the creation of this book with varying degrees of involvement stretching back to the winter of 2015-2016. My family, especially Krista, has supported me in this endeavor and has enriched my life incalculably. Our dear friend, Milly Butler, was the first person to read a complete draft of this study. She provided many useful suggestions to improve the readability of the book. Dennis Meeks and Charles Smith were kind enough to hand over their class at Compassion Christian Church for several weeks, during which time the group worked through *Reflections* with me. It was an honor to teach the material for the first time, and we had many fruitful discussions.

I appreciate those at Cascade Books who helped bring this study to print through the leadership of K. C. Hanson, as well as Dove McHargue for lending his talents for the cover design.

Introduction

I lost faith. I became the type of person my father warned me about: a Christian trained in secular higher education who no longer believed in the Christian message. Had my father been alive at the time, he would have been heart-broken. My wife was devastated. She informed me one day that this was not what she had signed up for. We met at Prairie Bible College in Alberta, Canada, several years before my crisis of faith. It is a conservative institution with a long history of training people who go on to serve in cross-cultural ministries. At the start of the fall semester, my wife met a college freshman who owned a high school letterman jacket that proudly proclaimed in large yellow letters: "Jesus is Alive!" That was me. Our first date was that spring at a concert by the Christian rock band known as Petra, famous for such songs as "Creed"—a strong statement of faith. Some thirteen months later, we were married. She fell in love with a dedicated Christ-follower; a man passionate about God and biblical studies. Now she found herself years later looking into the eyes of a man whom she still loved deeply, but whose spiritual life was so limited as to be nearly unnoticeable.

I was in a desolate and dark place. I did not sign up for this crisis either. I still went to church, but my faith was so far gone that at times I could not sing along during worship. Petra's "Creed" would have been impossible for me to express. I felt that a person should mean what they were singing, rather than simply go through the motions. That would be mere ritual, not devotion. Still I was going through some of the motions, such as attending services because I was not prepared to stop completely. I was trying. I was attempting to hold on to something that had been central to my life for years. I was very young, under six years old, when I first confessed my faith in Jesus Christ. I can still remember it now. I prayed with my father in a bedroom of our one story house in Brawley, California. It was the hottest and driest place that I have ever lived. The type of place where a shady spot was still 110°F. It is a desert town. Without the faith that started there, I found myself in a spiritual wilderness. It was dreary. I was thirsty. I was lost.

Thankfully, I was not alone. God and my wife remained close at hand. In fact, it was God working through my wife that helped keep me grounded. The darkest days of my crisis lasted for approximately a month. Such an amount of time sounds insignificant, but try holding your breath underwater for several minutes. Then tell me how it feels to be existing on a limited supply of a necessary ingredient for life, even if temporarily. I had distanced myself from the source of my spiritual life and I was struggling to live as intended.

Time is a strange phenomenon. Some moments pass with surprising speed, like the roller coaster ride you wait hours to experience. Other segments of time pass at an incremental pace, particularly when pain is involved. I am grateful that I was on the road to spiritual recovery after only a month of significant struggle, but it actually took me years to get to where I am today. Just as it took time to descend into disbelief, it was a steady climb to get to the place in which I could confidently "confess with [my] mouth Jesus *as* Lord, and believe in [my] heart that God raised Him from the dead" (Romans 10:9).[1]

We have just over a month to study the sacrificial death of Jesus together. It is a short period of time. I can neither say how quickly it will pass for you nor can I know where each of you are along the spectrum from disbelief to belief. You may be in a spiritual desert or firmly planted by streams of water, bearing much fruit (Psalm 1:3).[2] Wherever you are, the sacrifice of Christ is of

---

1. Unless otherwise noted, all Scripture quotations are taken from the New American Standard Bible. Some of these quotations have been reformatted for style, such as the removal of all caps.

2. Psalm 1:3—"And he will be like a tree *firmly* planted by streams of water,

such central importance that it mandates careful consideration and reflection. Forty days is not enough time to cover the topic completely, but it is a sufficient amount to make steady progress in reaching a richer understanding of how Jesus' death is represented in Scripture and what it means for us. I hope that these reflections will help you grow stronger in your faith. They have assisted me significantly. Let me tell you about the book.

Christmas Day was a fitting time to begin writing this study on the sacrificial death of Jesus, for it is a day to commemorate the earthly starting point of a life sent for a tremendous purpose. It is a day to focus upon Immanuel, the coming of God in the flesh to be with humanity, as prophesied thousands of years before the Nativity in the book of Isaiah (7:14).[3] When the Apostle Paul discussed the process of Jesus' incarnation (that is, becoming flesh) in Philippians 2, he explained it as a great act of humility in which the Son emptied himself in order to take on the form of a servant. Paul introduced the incarnation into the text to portray the right kind of mindset that should be found within Christians. Indeed, Jesus was brought forth in the text for the main reason of encouraging believers to be selfless as he was. In describing the selflessness of Christ, Paul demonstrated that Jesus emptied himself of his divine position to the end that he died by crucifixion in an act of humble obedience. Jesus was, in short, a willing participant in a mode of death feared and loathed by people in the Roman world. With few words the process of divine redemption was spelled out as a great act of selfless abandonment, leading first to human birth and then to execution.

The Christian narrative is more than simply about life and death, for it is a message of *sacrificial* suffering. It is about a willing surrendering of self to a bloody and excruciatingly painful process through which atonement was achieved. It is the purpose of this collection of reflections to encourage a better appreciation for the

---

which yields its fruit in its season, and its leaf does not wither; and in whatever he does, he prospers."

3. Isaiah 7:14—"Therefore the Lord Himself will give you a sign: Behold, a virgin will be with child and bear a son, and she will call His name Immanuel."

sacrifice of Christ as represented in the New Testament through examining the manner by which biblical authors presented the sacrificial process and its results. Jesus was crucified during the Jewish festival of Passover, linking his death to the ritual of spilling the blood of lambs in exchange for the lives of firstborn Israelites. Yet, the killing of Passover lambs does not represent the theological importance of Jesus' sacrificial work completely. In addition to Passover, the early church drew upon other biblical concepts when explaining that Jesus was both given by the Father and gave himself as a substitutionary carrier of iniquity on behalf of humanity. More specifically, the New Testament describes Jesus' sacrifice in conjunction with such things as Moses' elevation of a bronze serpent, sin-sacrifice, Day of Atonement rituals, heifer sacrifice, covenantal bloodshed, firstborn sacrifice, and the suffering of an Isaiah servant figure. Jesus' sacrificial death established a new covenant and brought about such key results as forgiveness, reconciliation, redemption, sanctification, and justification for believers. What is more, Jesus' death has served as a model for Christian behavior as his followers have sought or still seek to live daily in self-denial, bearing their crosses and denying their own aims for the sake of God's kingdom. For many in Christian history, self-denial has resulted in the ultimate price: martyrdom. Such a price is still being paid today by those who focus on eternal gains, rather than earthly longevity.

The sacrificial death of Christ is powerful, foundational, and necessary to the Christian faith. While much of the discussion in the pages that follow will focus upon the significance of Jesus' sacrifice, the resurrection of the Savior will not be forgotten. Easter Sunday recalls this glorious return to life, which, as Paul explained to the early church, was of central importance: without the resurrection, sin still reigns and the Christian faith has no merit. In other words, the sacrificial death accomplished nothing if the resurrection did not occur. Both are part of the process through which salvation was secured (1 Corinthians 15:3, 17).[4]

4. 1 Corinthians 15:3, 17—"For I delivered to you as of first importance what I also received, that Christ died for our sins according to the Scriptures

The following pages, then, provide a series of short reflections upon the sacrificial death and resurrection of Jesus as explained in several biblical texts. With the New Testament writers, we will encounter many concepts addressed in the Hebrew Bible (or Old Testament). The sacrificial death of Jesus cannot be understood adequately except in association with the first 39 books of the Bible. The Israelite sacrificial system was the primary context for Jesus and the early church in considering the means by which sin could be addressed. Blood, we shall see, was instrumental in the process. For the Israelites, life was contained in the blood (Genesis 9:4).[5] Ritually presenting the blood of a sacrificial victim was presenting the life. In a sense, there was an exchange: one life for the other. Sacrificial blood ceremonies had differing effects, one of which was atonement or the expiating of sin (Leviticus 17:11).[6]

For many Christians, particularly in the West, bloody sacrifice is far removed from daily life. I, for example, have only observed sacrifice on one occasion and it left a noticeable impression. In the late 1990s, I was provided with a unique opportunity to view the Samaritan Passover ceremony on the top of Mt. Gerizim, which is near Nablus in the West Bank/Israel. Whereas contemporary Judaism moved away from sacrifice in the wake of the Second Temple's destruction by the Romans in AD 70, the Samaritans brought Passover sacrifice into the modern era. When I share pictures from my experience with students, I sometimes warn them before showing the sacrificial procedures practiced by the Samaritans. Some may find the images of ritual slaughter disturbing—many people prefer to encounter meat in its packaged or cooked forms. After meeting the high priest, we watched as Samaritan men, who were ceremoniously dressed in white clothes, sacrificed sheep and prepared their bodies for cooking just a few feet in front of a very

---

. . . and if Christ has not been raised, your faith is worthless; you are still in your sins."

5. Genesis 9:4—"Only you shall not eat flesh with its life, *that is*, its blood."

6. Leviticus 17:11—"For the life of the flesh is in the blood, and I have given it to you on the altar to make atonement for your souls; for it is the blood by reason of the life that makes atonement."

interested crowd of onlookers. The event took place in a large open air plaza down the hill from where the Samaritans once had their own temple.

I cannot successfully imagine what it would have been like to observe such a horrific death as crucifixion in person. The sights, the sounds, and the smells of such a torturous form of execution are beyond me. Many of the Roman soldiers tasked with crucifying prisoners must have become desensitized over time to the anguish they inflicted. In Jesus' case, we can attempt to comprehend the sight of flowing blood from the open wounds of his whipping, as well as that dripping from the body parts punctured by thorns and nails. We can even try to consider what it would have been like to feel excruciating pain associated with those wounds and the deeply emotional strain of being largely abandoned by loved ones and followers, but it goes beyond most of our capacities to conceive. I do not believe that we are largely desensitized to the pain, like the Roman crucifier, but we are so removed from the time and place of first century Jerusalem that we cannot relate. Add to this the fact that we cannot appreciate what it was like to bear the sins of humanity, as Jesus did, and we are left with a limited understanding of what Jesus endured. For now, we look at things unclearly (1 Corinthians 13:12).[7] Please understand that I am not seeking to trivialize Christian suffering historically or in the contemporary era. Many have carried or still carry the marks of Jesus in their bodies due to persecution (Galatians 6:17).[8]

Many have known or now comprehend in a very literal manner what it is to deny self and to take up the cross, as Jesus directed (Mark 8:34–35).[9] This work is not about the significant suffering

7. 1 Corinthians 13:12—"For now we see in a mirror dimly, but then face to face; now I know in part, but then I shall know fully just as I also have been fully known."

8. Galatians 6:17—"From now on let no one cause trouble for me, for I bear on my body the brand-marks of Jesus."

9. Mark 8:34–35—"And He summoned the multitude with His disciples, and said to them, 'If anyone wishes to come after Me, let him deny himself, and take up his cross, and follow Me. For whoever wishes to save his life shall lose it; but whoever loses his life for My sake and the gospel's shall save it.'"

endured by so many, but it is primarily an attempt to better understand the theological significance of Jesus' sacrificial death as represented in the books bound together in the Bible.

Despite any inadequacies a person may have in appreciating the anguish of the cross, the biblical authors and the preserved words of Jesus have done much to help explain the nature of the sacrificial death in terms of how it should be interpreted. You are now invited to join me in a journey of reflection upon the biblical texts as we meditate upon the death of Jesus Christ and, to a much lesser extent, his resurrection. These thoughts are by no means exhaustive and they suffer from my own incomplete understanding of Jesus' sacrificial death. Still, it is my hope that you will gain a better appreciation for some of the many ways that his death is addressed in Scripture. Each of the following treatments is purposefully short, is based upon biblical analysis, and is meant to encourage self-reflection. Take your time and prayerfully consider the passages that are referenced. Find a quiet place. Underline meaningful verses. Memorize passages. Take notes in the book or write things down in a journal. Re-read the studies as needed. The more I have worked on this project, the more I have come to recognize how much I need it. Even if it is of no benefit to others, focusing on the scriptures related to the sacrificial death of Christ and the responses they demand has been a soothing relief to me. I have been challenged to live sacrificially and in a holier manner.

I

A Famous Chapter

Jesus answered and said to him, "Truly, truly, I say to you, unless one is born again, he cannot see the kingdom of God."

—JOHN 3:3

L et us begin this journey by thinking about the chapter in which one of the most famous verses of the New Testament appears. If its placement on signs at sporting events is any indication, John 3:16[1] must be one of the most often cited Christian texts. Its popularity likely stems from its concise statement of the Christian message or gospel: God's love prompted the giving of the Son and belief in him results in eternal life rather than eternal punishment. John 3:16 reflects core Christian beliefs so well with so few words that simply writing down a reference to it on a poster is seen as an evangelistic device. Just last night, my wife, children, and I saw such a use of John 3:16 painted on the trailer of a semi-truck travelling along the interstate. It prompted my wife, Krista, to lead a discussion with our sons about such a use of the verse. My sons, Alexander and Gabriel, are very familiar with the text. Christians introduce John 3:16 to children at an early age. It is, for example, the first memorization verse in the Awana Christian

1. John 3:16—"For God so loved the world, that He gave His only begotten Son, that whoever believes in Him should not perish, but have eternal life."

program for elementary school children. I was a Christian for a few years before I participated in Awana. It was the first time that I dedicated time to learning several biblical passages, which is an important discipline and one that I have not always practiced as well as I should.

Children learn about the sacrificial death of Jesus Christ as a means of forgiveness. Adults recognize the salvation process as an atoning work. The word *atonement* (or expiation) involves more than the idea of forgiveness. It primarily represents the concept that a sacrifice purges the impurity of sin.[i] This atonement secures forgiveness. John 3 does not explain the death of Jesus from the standpoint of atoning for sin, however. Such an idea is found elsewhere in Scripture and it will be discussed in the pages that follow. Still, John 3 describes Jesus' work with ritualistic and sacrificial concepts as we will see in this study and in the one that follows.

The primary focus of John 3 is a night encounter between Jesus and a Jewish religious leader by the name of Nicodemus— we, too, are on a journey of spiritual inquiry, seeking to meet with the Messiah or Christ. Jesus explained to Nicodemus that it was necessary for a person to be born anew. Nicodemus questioned such an idea, contemplating the impossibility of physical rebirth. Jesus went on to explain that the process of obtaining new life was a spiritual one. As the discussion unfolded, Jesus indicated that a person receives eternal life through belief. To demonstrate the notion of belief, Jesus drew upon a ritual from the days of Moses in which salvation in the form of healing was secured through gazing upon a raised figure.

Nicodemus would have been very familiar with the episode. It is told in Numbers 21. During the desert wandering days of early Israel, the people grew complacent and accused God and Moses of leading them to their deaths by starvation and dehydration. They were looking backwards towards Egypt and not forwards towards the land of promise (or Canaan). God responded by punishing the Israelites with a plague of serpents. After the people confessed their wrong and asked for Moses' intercession, Moses was instructed to place a replica of a serpent on a standard. Then those attacked by the venomous snakes lived simply by looking at the raised bronze serpent. This figure represented God's provision. Their gaze should have been focused on him and his provisions in the first place. Their complaining was a rejection of God's care (Numbers 21:5).[2]

Jesus informed Nicodemus that he must be raised up in a manner similar to the ritualistic uplifting of the bronze object of salvation (John 3:14–15).[3] This was a reference to his later crucifixion. Jesus was indicating that his death would have spiritual implications. He specified that those who place their faith in him will obtain eternal life, a process that requires more than the physical movement of the eyes, as in the bronze serpent situation. The Israelites lived by focusing their eyes on an object. While belief in the healing power of viewing the serpent was likely involved, Numbers 21 does not record that healing was based upon an internal response. Jesus, however, called for an inner reaction of faith in him, the one who was going to be lifted up to bring about salvation to the spiritually dying. Those poisoned by the venom of sin need to gaze upon the sacrificed Savior and respond in belief.

Reflection Questions

1. Have you been or are you currently in a desert place with a sense of physical or emotional exhaustion like the Israelites? How did you or are you responding?

2. In thinking about life's struggles, how often does your gaze focus upon difficult circumstances rather than upon God and heavenly provisions?

3. What type of response is required for those who regard the crucifixion of Jesus of Nazareth and what are some of the obstacles to belief?

2. Numbers 21:5—"And the people spoke against God and Moses, 'Why have you brought us up out of Egypt to die in the wilderness? For there is no food and no water, and we loathe this miserable food.'"

3. John 3:14–15—"And as Moses lifted up the serpent in the wilderness, even so must the Son of Man be lifted up; that whoever believes may in Him have eternal life."

2

A Famous Verse

For God so loved the world, that He gave His only begotten Son, that whoever believes in Him should not perish, but have eternal life.

—JOHN 3:16

John 3:16 does not explain Jesus' death in terms of ritual atonement, but the verse can be read as more explicitly sacrificial than it is normally considered. Indeed, the start of the verse can be translated to indicate that God the Father did not merely *give* his child, but that he gave the Son in a *sacrificial* manner. In this light, the verse could take on new meaning for English readers, and it has become a more meaningful verse to me. Such a translation would only necessitate the addition of a single word so that the beginning of the verse would indicate that God "*sacrificially gave*" the Son out of love for the human population. God "gave" his son or "sacrificially gave" his son are both valid translations of the Greek word (*didōmi*) rendered as "gave" in translations like the NASB and RSV.[ii] The idea of giving is the most common meaning of the word, but in certain contexts it can take on the additional idea of *giving in a sacrificial way* (see Leviticus 22:22[1] and Luke 2:24[2]).[iii]

Micah 6:6–8[3] is one of my favorite passages with its emphasis upon three key areas of righteous living and it is my ambition to live out its teachings. The prophet was guided to "practice justice, love kindness/steadfast love,[iv] and go forth humbly"[v] in his walk with God. These directives from God, which come in the form of a rhetorical question, were given in response to a series of questions posed in the preceding verses about how to gain divine approval within the confines of a sacrificial system. Within the list of potential sacrifices and offerings, such as offering rivers of oil, Micah wondered if he should go so far as to *give* his firstborn child to obtain forgiveness for sin. The Greek version of Micah 6:7 uses the same verb here as in John 3:16. The Hebrew, which is the passage's original language, similarly employs a common word for giving, but the context speaks about sacrifice. Micah asked if he should give his firstborn sacrificially. This is the only passage in the entire Hebrew Bible that explicitly explores the idea of child sacrifice for the forgiveness of sin. The innocent child would suffer for the sins of the father. Such an idea of substitutional suffering by a child to cleanse sin is neither endorsed in the passage nor elsewhere in the Hebrew Bible. God informed Micah that the proposed sacrifices and offerings were not necessary, but that a life characterized by performing justice, loving with a faithful love, and humbly following God corresponds to the ideal spiritual path.[vi]

---

1. Leviticus 22:22—"Those *that are* blind or fractured or maimed or having a running sore or eczema or scabs, you shall not offer to the Lord, nor make of them an offering by fire on the altar to the Lord."

2. Luke 2:24—"and to offer a sacrifice according to what was said in the Law of the Lord, 'A pair of turtle-doves, or two young pigeons.'"

3. Micah 6:6–8—"With what shall I come to the Lord and bow myself before the God on high? Shall I come to Him with burnt offerings, with yearling calves? Does the Lord take delight in thousands of rams, in ten thousand rivers of oil? Shall I present my first-born *for* my rebellious acts, the fruit of my body for the sin of my soul? He has told you, O man, what is good; and what does the Lord require of you but to do justice, to love kindness, and to walk humbly with your God?"

It is for the purpose of salvation, not judgement (John 3:17),[4] that a just Father, in an act of humble love, gave his Son sacrificially for the sake of humanity. Micah questioned whether his parental role would require sacrifice, but it did not. God himself, on the other hand, freely gave his Son in a sacrificial act not because God had done wrong, but due to humanity's breaching of the divine moral standard.

Let us pause here for we must guard ourselves from too quickly moving beyond the Father's role in the sacrificial narrative. Jesus was a willing victim (John 10:17–18),[5] but he died as a result of the Father's plan, direction, and will. For the next two days we will talk about the role of the Father, beginning by looking at an episode from the life of Abraham in which he was called to sacrifice his son Isaac, who was spared by substitution. As a father who almost lost a firstborn son in a backyard accident, I can relate to near loss and the joy of a recovered life, but I cannot comprehend sacrificing a child. The Father, however, orchestrated the sacrifice of his son. Scripture does not share how the Father felt at the time of Jesus' death. We are left to imagine. How do you think the Father reacted from an emotional standpoint?

Reflection Questions

1. How does a translation of John 3:16 that focuses on the sacrificial giving of the Son affect your understanding of the text (if it does)?

2. When you consider the sacrificial death of Jesus, do you tend to emphasize one person of the Trinity more than another? Why?

---

4. John 3:17—"For God did not send the Son into the world to judge the world, but that the world should be saved through Him."

5. John 10:17–18—"For this reason the Father loves Me, because I lay down My life that I may take it again. No one has taken it away from Me, but I lay it down on My own initiative. I have authority to lay it down, and I have authority to take it up again. This commandment I received from My Father."

3. Turn to Matthew 26:36–46. How does it relate to our discussion of John 3:16?

3

A Famous Verse and a Famous Narrative

For God so loved the world, that He gave His only begotten Son, that
whoever believes in Him should not perish, but have eternal life.

—JOHN 3:16

After these things, the following occurred: God tested Abraham
and said to him, "Abraham?" and he responded, "Here I am." Then
he said, "Take your only son, whom you adore, namely, Isaac; you,
yourself, travel to the land of Moriah, and send him up there as a
burnt-sacrifice upon one of the mountains which I will indicate
to you." Abraham woke up early in the morning, saddled his ass,
brought two of his young men along with him as well as Isaac, his
son; then he split the wood of the burnt-sacrifice, got up, and trav-
eled to the place where God indicated to him.

—GENESIS 22:1–3 [vii]

S everal years ago, I thought that I had detected an interesting
parallel between the sacrifice of Jesus and the near sacrifice
of Isaac; a biblical episode found in Genesis 22, which is known
as the *Akedah* or "Binding" in Jewish tradition because Isaac was
placed on the altar bound, but he was not killed. In the passage,

Isaac was forced to carry the wood for the burnt-sacrifice to the place of slaughter, just as Jesus carried the cross towards the place of crucifixion. It is intriguing, however, that the Gospels do not state such a correspondence explicitly. Indeed, I was surprised to learn through additional examination of the texts that the New Testament does not specifically point to parallels between Isaac and Jesus as much as I had anticipated. Abraham's role is emphasized more than Isaac's. In James 2:21–23[1] and Hebrews 11:17–19,[2] for example, Abraham's faith and the results of his attempt to sacrifice his son overshadow Isaac's participation as a victim in the ordeal. Still, Isaac is there and Jewish readers would likely have been quick to think about Abraham and Isaac when considering a father sacrificing a son. Genesis 22 is the most well-known human sacrificial narrative in the Hebrew Bible complete with a reference to animal substitution for the intended victim—we will consider the substitutionary nature of Jesus' sacrifice later.

Hebrews 11:17 states: "By faith Abraham, when he was tested, offered up Isaac; and he who had received the promises was offering up his only begotten *son*." The word translated as "only begotten" (*monogenēs*) is the same used to refer to Jesus in John 3:16. In fact, the writings associated with John use the term several times regarding Jesus (John 1:14, 18; 3:16, 18; 1 John 4:9).[3] When we turn to the beginning of Genesis 22, we see that Isaac is referenced as an only and beloved son. If John 3:16 intentionally points to

1. James 2:21–23—"Was not Abraham our father justified by works, when he offered up Isaac his son on the altar? You see that faith was working with his works, and as a result of the works, faith was perfected; and the Scripture was fulfilled which says, 'And Abraham believed God, and it was reckoned to him as righteousness,' and he was called the friend of God."

2. Hebrews 11:17–19—"By faith Abraham, when he was tested, offered up Isaac; and he who had received the promises was offering up his only begotten *son*; *it was he* to whom it was said, 'In Isaac your descendants shall be called.' He considered that God is able to raise *men* even from the dead; from which he also received him back as a type."

3. See, for example, John 1:14 and 18—"And the Word became flesh, and dwelt among us, and we beheld His glory, glory as of the only begotten from the Father, full of grace and truth . . . No man has seen God at any time; the only begotten God, who is in the bosom of the Father, He has explained *Him*."

9

Genesis 22, which is a valid perspective,[viii] then it is fascinating to consider the way that love is mentioned in John in contrast to Genesis. Abraham was called to sacrifice the son he loved,[ix] whereas God gave his only Son sacrificially out of love for the entire world. Jesus is called the Father's beloved in the New Testament (Matthew 3:17)[4] and the Father's love for him is mentioned in John 3:35,[5] but the focus of John 3:16 is a much more expansive love in terms of the recipients.

Micah considered the need to sacrifice his firstborn for his sins, but was not required to do so. Abraham nearly sacrificed his son, but a substitution was provided. God the Father went through with the sacrifice. Why?

Reflection Questions

1. According to John 3:16, why did the Father sacrifice Jesus?

2. How does John 3:16 explain the greatness of the Father's love in comparison to the love Abraham had for his son?

3. What kind of response does the love found in John 3:16 evoke in you?

---

4. Matthew 3:17—"and behold, a voice out of the heavens, saying, 'This is My beloved Son, in whom I am well-pleased.'"

5. John 3:35—"The Father loves the Son, and has given all things into His hand."

4

A Parallel to a Famous Verse and the Source of Love

> By this the love of God was manifested in us, that God has sent His
> only begotten Son into the world so that we might live through Him.
> In this is love, not that we loved God, but that He loved us and sent
> His Son *to be* the propitiation for our sins. Beloved, if God so loved
> us, we also ought to love one another.
>
> —1 JOHN 4:9–11

The terminology and ideas found in 1 John 4 demonstrate a
clear correspondence to John 3. Both speak to divine love,
the sending of the Son, Jesus' status as "only begotten," and the
possibility of obtaining life as a result of the Son's entrance into
worldly affairs. As previously noted, John 3 is not about a sacrifice for sin, but 1 John 4:10 does provide such a concept. The key
phrase is translated above as "the propitiation for our sins." The
word translated as "propitiation" (*hilasmos*) is used in the ancient
Greek translation of the Hebrew Bible for references to atonement,
forgiveness, and sin-offering.[x] In short, 1 John 4:10 indicates that
the Son was sent by the Father for the purpose of being a sacrifice
that atones or expiates sin.

The verse explains that the very model of love is embodied by
the twofold activity of the Father:

1. God loved even when there was a lack of human reciprocity; and

2. He sent the Son to secure expiation/atonement for sin.

That is the type of love behind John 3:16. Later 1 John 4 explains that God himself equals love (v. 16) [1] and that our love derives from God loving us first (v. 19). *The source and model of sacrificial love is God himself!* But there is more. Our response to God's love must result in loving each other (v. 11). Hatred for others demonstrates a lack of God's love in us. The two cannot inhabit the same space (vv. 20–21).[2] My life has room for more of God's love to reside.

Reflection Questions

1. What is the source of love and how has it been manifested in the world most significantly?

2. How does God's love compel us to respond?

3. In terms of personal relationships, where do you need a greater outpouring of God's love?

1. 1 John 4:16—"And we have come to know and have believed the love which God has for us. God is love, and the one who abides in love abides in God, and God abides in him."

2. 1 John 4:20–21—"If someone says, 'I love God,' and hates his brother, he is a liar; for the one who does not love his brother whom he has seen, cannot love God whom he has not seen. And this commandment we have from Him, that the one who loves God should love his brother also."

5

An Atoning Advocate

My little children, I am writing these things to you that you may not sin. And if anyone sins, we have an Advocate with the Father, Jesus Christ the righteous; and He Himself is the propitiation for our sins; and not for ours only, but also for *those of* the whole world. And by this we know that we have come to know Him, if we keep His commandments . . . but whoever keeps His word, in him the love of God has truly been perfected. By this we know that we are in Him: the one who says he abides in Him ought himself to walk in the same manner as He walked.

—1 JOHN 2:1–3, 5–6

As with the previous study, the same terminology occurs when speaking about Jesus' role as "the propitiation for our sins"; indeed, this passage is the only other appearance of the same Greek word (*hilasmos*) in the New Testament. Importantly, the focus is different: rather than 1 John 4's emphasis upon the sacrifice of Christ serving to atone for the sins of the Christian community, chapter 2 designates a broader application of the expiating work. *It applies to sins around the world.* The focus is not upon addressing the sins of a particular community or nation, as in the Israelite Day of Atonement, but any individual's sin, mine, and yours. As emphasized here and in John 3:16, the role of Jesus Christ as Savior has global implications. His was not a messianic undertaking for a small group of people, but a movement that has transcended ethnic, racial, and national lines (see Acts 1:8).[1]

From the standpoint of divine judgement, iniquity must be addressed lest the sinner incur the penalty meted out by a just and holy God. 1 John 2 transports the reader to a scene in the heavens. There the righteous Father presides over the judgement of sin, and when a follower of Jesus transgresses God's moral standards, then Jesus stands in as a representative or advocate for the errant one.[xi] Jesus represents his or her interests as one who addressed the sin committed. The penalty is, therefore, not applied to the believer. The passage is reminiscent of Romans 8:1,[2] which indicates that believers are free from condemnation. Christ's work is not to be taken for granted as if belief in him were a license to sin. As the end of the above scriptural quotation indicates, obeying Jesus' teaching demonstrates the development of divine love in the believer. The sign of the authentic Christian walk is conformity to the ways of Jesus. As we mature in Christ, we should be sinning less and loving more. 1 John 2 even explains that the text was written to help young or immature Christians cease sinning; yet the passage provides hope should transgression occur. There is a trustworthy advocate!

A few years ago I required a human advocate to represent me before a judge for a traffic violation. I transgressed the law and was guilty of speeding. Instead of paying the fine for the ticket I received while on a trip, I asked a local court official to represent my interests in court because the violation occurred a significant distance from my home. Some human advocates are great, others are not. Mine was not. The person was absent-minded and forgot to advocate on my behalf. I phoned after the court date to learn of the error and mentioned that I hoped a bench warrant had not

1. Acts 1:8—"'but you shall receive power when the Holy Spirit has come upon you; and you shall be My witnesses both in Jerusalem, and in all Judea and Samaria, and even to the remotest part of the earth.'"

2. Romans 8:1—"There is therefore now no condemnation for those who are in Christ Jesus."

been issued against me. The representative indicated that one had not *yet* been issued. The official quickly resolved the matter by contacting the chief of police. I paid the fee and attended a defensive driving course, which avoided a visit to my home by the sheriff's department because I did not appear before the judge. I trusted the advocate, who guided me in taking the appropriate steps in the legal process. I did my part but at the pivotal moment, the official neglected to take up my interests.

Thankfully, we do not have an absent-minded and negligent representative in the heavens. Jesus stands ready to advocate on my behalf. I can have total confidence in him. I cannot say the same for human representatives. A key component of Christ's advocacy is that he already addressed my guilt. He is the expiation for my wrong-doing. He is righteous, as this passage explains. I am only righteous through him.

Reflection Questions

1. How does 1 John 2 represent the atoning work of Jesus differently than 1 John 4?

2. What hope does 1 John 2 provide for the believer?

3. In what ways are you most thankful for an advocate and what practical steps can you take to require the advocacy of Christ less in those areas?

6

Giving Himself Sacrificially

For the grace of God has appeared, bringing salvation to all men, instructing us to deny ungodliness and worldly desires and to live sensibly, righteously and godly in the present age, looking for the blessed hope and the appearing of the glory of our great God and Savior, Christ Jesus; who gave Himself for us, that He might redeem us from every lawless deed and purify for Himself a people for His own possession, zealous for good deeds.

—TITUS 2:11–14

We have observed so far the sacrificial giving of Jesus by the Father to secure widespread salvation. In this study the focus shifts from the actions of the Father in the sacrificial process to the victim's role in sacrificing himself. When Titus 2 indicates that Jesus "gave Himself for us," the same Greek word found in John 3:16 is employed to designate the sacrificial act: Jesus sacrificially gave himself. The Gospel narratives recount Jesus' submission to the Father's will in the Garden of Gethsemane on the night of his trial and arrest (Matthew 26:36–46; Mark 14:32–42; Luke 22:39–46).[1] Jesus certainly did not take the situation lightly, asking repeatedly that should it be possible, he wished that the Father would release

1. For example, Luke 22:42—"saying, 'Father, if Thou art willing, remove this cup from Me; yet not My will, but Thine be done.'"

him from the approaching ordeal. The unwritten answer was that it must be accomplished. Also on that night, Jesus is remembered for having said: "Greater love has no one than this, that one lay down his life for his friends" (John 15:13). Jesus, motivated by love, submitted to the heavenly mandate and gave himself sacrificially in a death by crucifixion.

Titus 2 explains that Jesus did this for two reasons. First, his goal was to redeem people from unlawful acts. This verse is not focusing on Roman legal standards, but upon divinely-oriented law. Jesus gave himself to redeem people from every type of transgression against God's moral code. Second, Jesus sacrificially delivered himself for the purpose of cleansing a group of people, who would be considered his possession. Both the idea of a people as Jesus' property and the notion of redemption speak to the concept of purchasing.[xii] A monetary transaction was not the intended meaning; rather, the verse describes the exchange of Jesus' life to secure redemption and cleansing.

The verse ends with an indication that these people would zealously perform good things, which is one of the reasons that they were purchased. The phrase at the end of the above biblical quotation ("zealous for good deeds") could evoke in an early Christian reader the concept of a Zealot. One of Jesus' disciples was so identified (Luke 6:15).[2] A Zealot in ancient Palestine, as is widely recognized, was a political revolutionary intent on the overthrow of Roman authority. Such a political revolutionary is not what Titus 2 has in mind, but it might help us to consider that the followers of Jesus are meant for a life of revolutionary good. It is our purpose to be involved in doing good. It is what we were created for (Ephesians 2:10).[3] We must be as passionate about doing the types of positive things that, with God's help, will dramatically overthrow oppression in our societies as the Zealots were about

---

2. Luke 6:15—"and Matthew and Thomas; James *the son* of Alphaeus, and Simon who was called the Zealot."

3. Ephesians 2:10—"For we are His workmanship, created in Christ Jesus for good works, which God prepared beforehand, that we should walk in them."

revolutionizing theirs. We must be revolutionary doers of good things; zealous about the kingdom of heaven.

Within the kingdom of God, things do not operate as they do when humans set the standards. Jesus was the great social revolutionary of his time, breaking societal norms in pursuing good things. He taught, for example, "You have heard that it was said, 'You shall love your neighbor, and hate your enemy.' But I say to you, love your enemies, and pray for those who persecute you" (Matthew 5:43–44). This is a tall order. My natural inclination is to hold a grudge against those who wrong me. Jesus promoted the practice of doing the unexpected, such as going the extra mile, which is literally what he communicated in Matthew 5:41.[4] We need to go beyond societal expectations in passionately doing good things.

Reflection Questions

1. In what ways are Titus 2 and John 3 different in explaining the sacrificial nature of Jesus' death?

2. According to Titus 2, what goals motivated Jesus' sacrifice?

3. Are we more often motivated by God-oriented passion or a sense of duty when it comes to good works? How do the actions of Christ as explained in today's study inspire us to act?

4. Matthew 5:41—"And whoever shall force you to go one mile, go with him two."

7

Grace and Salvation

For the grace of God has appeared, bringing salvation to all men, instructing us to deny ungodliness and worldly desires and to live sensibly, righteously and godly in the present age, looking for the blessed hope and the appearing of the glory of our great God and Savior, Christ Jesus; who gave Himself for us, that He might redeem us from every lawless deed and purify for Himself a people for His own possession, zealous for good deeds.

—TITUS 2:11–14

In the preceding study, I chose to examine the last part of the passage presented because of its link to previous material, but I am compelled to reflect upon the ideas expressed in the first two-thirds of the quotation, particularly the notion of grace. Grace is one of the greatest aspects in the relationship between God and humanity, and it is also found in human to human relations. Important for our purposes is that it is intimately linked to the sacrificial death of Christ. Having grown up in the church, my mind easily turns to an often cited definition of grace. Perhaps you have heard a variation of it, but the word is taken as an acronym in English to be: "God's Riches at Christ's Expense." This clever and generally accepted idea is not exactly a biblical definition, but it actually corresponds in part to one verse about grace rather well.

19

Second Corinthians 8:9 reads: "For you know the grace of our Lord Jesus Christ, that though He was rich, yet for your sake He became poor, that you through His poverty might become rich." Still, the acronym does not capture the basic concept of grace. The writings of Paul are particularly filled with references to grace; the word for grace (*charis*) appears around 100 times in his epistles, as in the verse just noted. One of the more commonly known passages about grace appears in Paul's letter to the Ephesian church. In Ephesians 2:8–9, one reads: "For by grace you have been saved through faith; and that not of yourselves, *it is* the gift of God; not as a result of works, that no one should boast." These verses relate to another commonly held view of grace, that is, it is something given from God that is unmerited. While grace is undeserved, reducing it to God's generous gifts does not quite get to the basic meaning.

The idea of favor captures the essence of grace (*charis*) well. This can be gathered by considering the following: James 4:6 reads, "But He gives a greater grace. Therefore *it* says: 'God is opposed to the proud, but gives grace to the humble.'" This verse quotes from the Greek version of Proverbs 3:34. Where the Greek of Proverbs 3:34 uses *charis*, the Hebrew word is *ḥēn*, which in many instances relates to the concept of finding favor in someone's eyes. Genesis 6:8 presents an example of this idea when it states that Noah was viewed in a favorable light by God. Indeed, "favor" is one of the ways that the idea of grace is translated in the Bible. This is how the Hebrew is translated in Genesis 6:8[1] or how the Greek is rendered in Luke 1:30 by several translations (RSV, ESV, and NASB). One of these reads: "And the angel said to her, 'Do not be afraid, Mary; for you have found favor with God.'"

Applying this understanding to Titus 2:11–14, one could say that God's favor burst forth to achieve humanity's salvation, "instructing us to deny ungodliness and worldly desires and to live sensibly, righteously and godly in the present age, looking for the blessed hope and the appearing of the glory of our great God and Savior, Christ Jesus." These verses explain how God's grace instructs me to live in my current circumstances. As I anticipate the

---

1. Genesis 6:8—"But Noah found favor in the eyes of the Lord."

return of Christ, I am to conduct myself in a way that is filled with good-sense, upright living, and godly behavior. I can only do so by the grace or favor of God.

Reflection Questions

1. How do you understand grace?
2. What has grace accomplished?
3. How does grace instruct us to live and how are you doing in those areas?

8

Giving Himself Sacrificially for a Ransom

First of all, then, I urge that entreaties *and* prayers, petitions *and* thanksgivings, be made on behalf of all men, for kings and all who are in authority, in order that we may lead a tranquil and quiet life in all godliness and dignity. This is good and acceptable in the sight of God our Savior, who desires all men to be saved and to come to the knowledge of the truth. For there is one God, *and* one mediator also between God and men, *the* man Christ Jesus, who gave Himself as a ransom for all, the testimony *borne* at the proper time.

—1 TIMOTHY 2:1–6

The above quotation begins with the instruction that all people, but particularly those in positions of power, should be the focus of intercession so that peace might be achieved. This is followed shortly thereafter by the expression of a divine desire for the salvation of every person. Such an all-inclusive focus is in line with what we have seen so far. It was after all God's love for the entire world that motivated the sacrificial giving of the Son. As in a previous study, the focus of the sacrificial giving in today's passage is upon the victim,[xiii] Jesus, as an active agent in his own death. It was a sacrifice that served as payment for everyone. Notice that the passage indicates that the ransom purposefully addressed everyone, but that all had not experienced salvation. There is a sufficiency in the sacrifice, but it must receive belief at the individual level.

Reference is made here to Jesus' humanity and the oneness of God. With my students, I have on occasion referred to Christianity as having a complex monotheism, that is, a complex belief in the oneness of God. The fundamental view of our faith is in a Trinitarian monotheism in which God's nature is regarded as consisting of one God in three persons, called God the Father, God the Son, and God the Holy Spirit. This means that Jesus' humanity is the result of the incarnation, that is, God becoming flesh by exceptional means: a virgin's impregnation without sexual intercourse. To defend Jesus' divinity, while acknowledging his humanity, the church produced the Nicene Creed centuries after Jesus' birth. The concepts of the creed are derived from scriptural interpretation. Both the humanity and divinity of Jesus are articulated in the New Testament. A passage that speaks to both was mentioned in the introduction to this book. Philippians 2:5–8 reads:

> Have this attitude in yourselves which was also in Christ Jesus, who, although He existed in the form of God, did not regard equality with God a thing to be grasped, but emptied Himself, taking the form of a bond-servant, *and* being made in the likeness of men. And being found in appearance as a man, He humbled Himself by becoming obedient to the point of death, even death on a cross.

Jesus, himself, is remembered for having referenced his divine nature and oneness with the Father (John 8:58;[1] 10:30).[2] In this regard, then, there is no conflict between stating that both Jesus and the Father were active in the sacrifice. Being divine and human, Jesus is uniquely placed to represent God to humans and humans to God.

First Timothy 2:5 describes Jesus as a mediator. The role of a mediator is to bring two sides together to promote a peaceful

1. John 8:58—"Jesus said to them, 'Truly, truly, I say to you, before Abraham was born, I am.'"

2. John 10:30—"I and the Father are one."

coexistence. Elsewhere the New Testament specifies that Jesus is the means by which peace with God is achieved (Romans 5:1),[3] and in another passage about the divinity of Christ, it states: "For it was the *Father's* good pleasure for all the fullness to dwell in Him, and through Him to reconcile all things to Himself, having made peace through the blood of His cross; through Him, *I say*, whether things on earth or things in heaven" (Colossians 1:19–20). Blood was a necessary component of the peace process because it was the substance that addressed the sin that created the breach in the relationship between God and his creations.

Reflection Questions

1. How is God's desire in terms of salvation represented in 1 Timothy 2:3–6?

2. How is it possible that Jesus and the Father were both active in giving sacrificially?

3. How does Jesus' role as mediator impact you?

3. Romans 5:1—"Therefore having been justified by faith, we have peace with God through our Lord Jesus Christ."

9

Giving Himself Sacrificially for a Ransom (Again)

And calling them to Himself, Jesus said to them, "You know that those who are recognized as rulers of the Gentiles lord it over them; and their great men exercise authority over them. But it is not so among you, but whoever wishes to become great among you shall be your servant; and whoever wishes to be first among you shall be slave of all. For even the Son of Man did not come to be served, but to serve, and to give His life a ransom for many."

—MARK 10:42–45 (SEE MATTHEW 20:25–28)

Jesus demonstrated in this passage an aspect of his role as a social revolutionary, that is, he expressed a mode of leadership that went against the norm in terms of positions of power. The wider context of the discourse is that Jesus was on his final trip to Jerusalem with his followers. Having told the disciples that he was going to be tortured and killed in Jerusalem, two disciples (John and James) approached their master with a special request. They wanted to be granted the two highest positions of power next to Jesus when he becomes glorified. Jesus told the brothers that it was not his place to fulfill such a request. Upon hearing of the exchange, the other disciples were understandably upset. The boldness of the brothers was not appreciated. I would think that there was some jealously involved—I probably would have been. In any case, Jesus drew upon the typical form of authority operating in the area to present a contrast with the style of leadership that was best.

Jesus and his disciples were under the rule of the Roman occupiers. The disciples did not need to imagine how Roman authority worked—they lived under its shadow every day. Jesus once encountered a Roman leader (Luke 7) who explained the power dynamics well. A centurion noted that the chain of command had a top down effect. When he gave a command, those under him did what he said (Luke 7:8).[1] In short, the person in the inferior position served the one above him or her. Jesus turned this model upside down, noting that serving others is what true leaders should do. These would be empty words had Jesus not modeled such leadership. He indicated that it was not his place to sit around and receive the service of others; rather, it was his goal to give himself sacrificially (*didōmi*) for the purpose of ransoming many people. Such a perspective takes service to a whole new level and goes against the norm of the leadership style that people were expecting from the Messiah, who was chiefly expected to overthrow Rome and establish a political kingdom.

It is worthwhile to consider that when one of the disciples, who learned this lesson from Jesus, wrote about the nature of church leadership, he advised the shepherds not to rule over their flocks in a domineering manner, but to live as examples. This is the same message Jesus taught and modeled for the writer, namely, Peter (1 Peter 5:1-3).[2]

1. Luke 7:8—"For I, too, am a man under authority, with soldiers under me; and I say to this one, 'Go!' and he goes; and to another, 'Come!' and he comes; and to my slave, 'Do this!' and he does it."

2. 1 Peter 5:1-3—"Therefore, I exhort the elders among you, as *your* fellow elder and witness of the sufferings of Christ, and a partaker also of the glory that is to be revealed, shepherd the flock of God among you, exercising oversight not under compulsion, but voluntarily, according to *the will of* God; and not for sordid gain, but with eagerness; nor yet as lording it over those allotted to your charge, but proving to be examples to the flock."

Reflection Questions

1. If the people of Jesus' day were mainly looking for a messianic leader who would rule in a political office as king, how easily do you think people would have received the message of a suffering servant leader?

2. What is the common style of leadership that you most frequently encounter, expect, or practice?

3. Do you feel more empowered or less by serving others?

I O

Giving Himself Sacrificially (Again)

Paul, an apostle (not *sent* from men, nor through the agency of man,
but through Jesus Christ, and God the Father, who raised Him from
the dead), and all the brethren who are with me, to the churches of
Galatia: Grace to you and peace from God our Father, and the Lord
Jesus Christ, who gave Himself for our sins, that He might deliver
us out of this present evil age, according to the will of our God and
Father, to whom *be* the glory forevermore. Amen.

—GALATIANS 1:1–5

S everal years ago, the University of Michigan prepared a display
on the history of biblical manuscripts. It was an impressive representation of texts, including a copy of the *Gutenberg Bible* and,
if I recall correctly, a 1611 *King James Bible*. The transmission and
preservation of the Bible over the centuries is remarkable and digi-
tization efforts have greatly aided not only in preservation but accessibility. One can, for example, read some of the earliest biblical
texts, the Dead Sea Scrolls, from the convenience of anywhere you
can get an internet connection. Still, seeing an ancient manuscript
in person is a sight to behold. The visit to the Michigan graduate
library display was memorable. I am most fond of the opportunity
I had to view some of Galatians from the early papyrus text called
P46.[xiv]

As a professor, I have often read some of the opening line of the papyrus page to my students, but I have not been giving Galatians chapter 1 much thought from a sacrificial standpoint. The idea of Jesus giving himself sacrificially (*didōmi*) is found therein. It parallels several of the passages already examined in our studies. Here, verse four specifies that Jesus performed such a sacrifice to address sin with the purpose of securing the removal or deliverance of his followers from a time characterized by evil. This was done in line with the Father's will. These five verses, which are presented as a salutary prayer, provide a concise overview of the essence of the Christian message, but not as briefly as John 3:16.

As you read the remainder of chapter 1 of Galatians, you can see Paul was concerned that the Galatians had been following a message that diverged from the gospel he previously preached to them. A key issue addressed in Galatians was whether or not non-Jewish male Christians were bound by the Jewish commandment to be circumcised; the book of Galatians more broadly considers the applicability of the Law or Mosaic Covenant to Christians. Paul's perspective is summarized in Galatians 3:13–14: "Christ redeemed us from the curse of the Law, having become a curse for us—for it is written, 'Cursed is everyone who hangs on a tree'—in order that in Christ Jesus the blessing of Abraham might come to the Gentiles, so that we might receive the promise of the Spirit through faith." This act of redemption is described at the start of the letter by indicating that Jesus sacrificially died to address sin. These verses from chapter 3 focus upon the highly negative connotations of dying by means of crucifixion. Not only was it physically agonizing. It was also spiritually undesirable.

When looking at chapters 2 and 3 of Galatians, we can see Paul's argument that keeping the principles of the Law of Moses, like circumcision and dietary restrictions, would not achieve a correct standing with God; rather, such a standing could only be gained through faith. Remember, faith was the standard that went back before the Mosaic Covenant to the one with Abraham. While Paul emphasized the relationship between the Gentiles and the gospel, his perspective applied to Jews, too. It was unnecessary for Christians (Jewish or non-Jewish) to adhere to the Law and, thus, follow Jewish customs. According to Paul, racial and other relational categories were erased in Jesus: Jew and Greek were no longer distinguished.

Reflection Questions

1. A big struggle I have had in my personal theology is that I have gotten too caught up with a law-oriented approach to God. How is that true for you?

2. Take the time to skim through Deuteronomy 27 to find out more regarding the Mosaic Covenant and the idea of curses. How does that help in understanding Galatians 3:13–14?

3. If you are a non-Jewish Christian, how does this study help you appreciate your inclusion into the line of Abraham? Read Galatians 3:23–29 for more information.

11

More about the Law, Faith, and Sacrificial Giving

But if, while seeking to be justified in Christ, we ourselves have also been found sinners, is Christ then a minister of sin? May it never be! For if I rebuild what I have *once* destroyed, I prove myself to be a transgressor. For through the Law, I died to the Law, that I might live to God. I have been crucified with Christ; and it is no longer I who live, but Christ lives in me; and the *life* which I now live in the flesh I live by faith in the Son of God, who loved me, and delivered Himself up for me. I do not nullify the grace of God; for if righteousness *comes* through the Law, then Christ died needlessly.

—GALATIANS 2:17–21

The focus of this day's study is upon Paul's view of Jewish Law in comparison to faith in Jesus' sacrificial death, which is described here with a word (*paradidōmi*) to indicate that Jesus "delivered Himself up" (NASB) or, more poignantly, "gave himself up sacrificially."[xv] I am not Jewish, but I am very fond of Jewish culture and I have a true interest in Jewish traditions. Over the years, I have spent meaningful time with Jewish Israelis and Jews living elsewhere. I have had meaningful experiences at Messianic Synagogues, which are places of worship for Jews who believe that Jesus is the Messiah. Messianic Jews constitute a stream of broader Christianity. They are Jewish Christians who emphasize their Jewish heritage in services. If you have not visited such a congregation, I highly recommend it. Worship times are open to non-Jewish Christians as well.

The idea of Messianic Judaism is a bit of a complicated concept because there are and have been different forms of messianism over the years. The most recognizable non-Christian messianic movement is represented by belief in Rebbe Menachem Mendel Schneerson, who died in 1994. I recall well the large poster of him that was hanging in the Jewish Quarter of the Old City of Jerusalem in the late 1990s, which mentioned the belief in his position as Messiah and king. His followers have blanketed modern-day Israel with signage, promoting him.

There is actually no distinction between the two concepts of king and Messiah from a biblical standpoint, that is, God's anointed one (or Messiah) was the king. "Christ" is derived from the Greek equivalent to the Hebrew word for Messiah. Thus, the statement "Jesus Christ" is like saying "Jesus Messiah." Christ is his title and not his last name, as friends of mine once asked me. The messianic movement of Jesus Christ, that is, the entire Christian faith, is the largest messianic following in the world.

We, as Jewish and non-Jewish Christians, believe that Jesus came in fulfillment of messianic promises brought forth in the Hebrew Bible about a coming king. The Davidic Covenant (2 Samuel 7) with its promise that David will always have a descendent to reign on his throne is the foundation of this type of messianism (v. 16).[1]

My family and I were graciously welcomed and included in a service at a local Messianic Christian congregation. Their service was both a mix of what you would find in a non-Jewish Christian service, as well as what is evident in a non-Christian Jewish meeting. It is a beautiful blend. One of their practices, which is also in mainstream Judaism, is reverence for the Torah Scroll—such

---

1. 2 Samuel 7:16—"And your house and your kingdom shall endure before Me forever; your throne shall be established forever."

a scroll is a copy of the text of the first five books of the Bible, also known as the Torah or Law (Genesis through Deuteronomy). During a service, the Torah Scroll is paraded through the congregation and it is also read. Prior to dismissing the children for Shabbat School (like Sunday School), the rabbi called the children forward to teach them a lesson and to perform a blessing over them. I quickly turned to my youngest son, Gabriel, and informed him that he was NOT to touch the scroll. I am not sure about this particular congregation, but the general practice in Judaism is that human hands are not to touch the text. My son went forward, climbed up on the stage near the scroll, AND climbed back down without touching the scroll. My heart must have skipped a few beats. My wife, Krista, and possibly others in the congregation felt the same way. My son wanted to see what this sacred text looked like and I can understand his curiosity—remember my fondness with seeing the papyrus from the book of Galatians? Thankfully, no damage was done and the rabbi even extended an open-ended invitation to worship with them again.

When Paul wrote about the Law or Torah, he could use it in reference to the five books or to the commandments of the Mosaic Covenant found in those books (see 1 Corinthians 9:8–9, 20).[2] Paul noted that he was particularly zealous about Jewish traditions (Galatians 1:14)[3] and was once part of a group that specialized in the Law, called the Pharisees. Like people of today, Paul would have exercised respect when handling a sacred text of Scripture. He did not take his faith lightly and believed that if a person could be saved by their works, then he had a very good shot at it

---

2. 1 Corinthians 9:8–9, 20—"I am not speaking these things according to human judgment, am I? Or does not the Law also say these things? For it is written in the Law of Moses, 'You shall not muzzle the ox while he is threshing.' God is not concerned about oxen, is He? . . . And to the Jews I became as a Jew, that I might win Jews; to those who are under the Law, as under the Law, though not being myself under the Law, that I might win those who are under the Law."

3. Galatians 1:14—"and I was advancing in Judaism beyond many of my contemporaries among my countrymen, being more extremely zealous for my ancestral traditions."

(Philippians 3:4–6).[4] He did not believe it to be the case. The Law, he believed, was necessary, yet insufficient. He said, "Therefore the Law has become our tutor *to lead us* to Christ, that we may be justified by faith. But now that faith has come, we are no longer under a tutor" (Galatians 3:24–25).

In the passage presented at the start of today's study, Paul recognized that true life resulted from faith in the person who loved Paul deeply and sacrificially gave himself up on his behalf in order that Paul might have life. Elsewhere, Paul explained to the church at Colossae that Christ is literally life for the Christian (Colossians 3:3–4).[5]

Reflection Questions

1. In what ways has legalism crept into your life or that of the church?

2. How do you think that the Law acted as a tutor for Paul? (Read Romans 7:7)

3. In a previous study, we encountered a passage about how we are to perform good things zealously. When does such activity cross the line into a work-based relationship with God in which God's grace is diminished in favor of seeking divine approval through the positive things we do?

---

4. Philippians 3:4–6—"although I myself might have confidence even in the flesh. If anyone else has a mind to put confidence in the flesh, I far more: circumcised the eighth day, of the nation of Israel, of the tribe of Benjamin, a Hebrew of Hebrews; as to the Law, a Pharisee; as to zeal, a persecutor of the church; as to the righteousness which is in the Law, found blameless."

5. Colossians 3:3–4—"For you have died and your life is hidden with Christ in God. When Christ, who is our life, is revealed, then you also will be revealed with Him in glory."

12

Law vs. Grace

But if, while seeking to be justified in Christ, we ourselves have also been found sinners, is Christ then a minister of sin? May it never be! For if I rebuild what I have *once* destroyed, I prove myself to be a transgressor. For through the Law, I died to the Law, that I might live to God. I have been crucified with Christ; and it is no longer I who live, but Christ lives in me; and the *life* which I now live in the flesh I live by faith in the Son of God, who loved me, and delivered Himself up for me. I do not nullify the grace of God; for if righteousness *comes* through the Law, then Christ died needlessly.

—GALATIANS 2:17–21

Paul acknowledged the importance of grace and the inadequacies of the Law in producing righteousness in contrast to what was accomplished through the death of Jesus. There is a tension between the Law and God's grace. Recall Ephesians 2:8–9 from a previous study? The verses read: "For by grace you have been saved through faith; and that not of yourselves, *it is* the gift of God; not as a result of works, that no one should boast." Grace and faith stand on one side and the Law and works on the other.

I am reminded of a unique experience I had several months ago. I was given the opportunity to return to Israel for a short trip on behalf of my university. Many things changed during the 15 year interlude between when my wife and I were blessed to live there and my recent visit. The most notable difference is the large wall and fence barrier system, separating the West Bank from Israel. Much had not changed, however. For instance, the afternoon stroll I took to our old neighborhood in Jerusalem led me to the corner market where we often purchased challah bread, a Shabbat staple. To my surprise, the same shopkeeper was there, aged but unmoved from the spot I remembered. I similarly spent time reacquainting myself with our old friends who worked in the Old City's Christian Quarter. We are all older and, perhaps wiser now, but our relationship continued as if unaffected by the distance of time and place. During my return flight from Tel Aviv, I made a new acquaintance.

As I sat on the flight home reading a book about parenting with grace, I could not help but notice a stark contrast between my book and the reading material chosen by the man next to me. I observed by their dress code that he and his wife were very pious Jews, seeking to live out the Law as interpreted through the lens of Haredi Judaism (what some people call Ultra-Orthodox Judaism). There I sat, trying to learn more about grace, and there he was, seeking to comprehend the legal traditions better, reading from a book that appeared to be the Talmud or Mishnah.[xvi] Through our introduction, I learned that the man seated next to me was named Moshe (or Moses), which is a strong name harkening back to the prophet associated with giving the Law. It is also a fitting name because of the nature of our encounter. I could have been sitting next to Paul in his days when he was known as Saul, that is, when he was seeking to be righteous through the legal traditions as a devout Pharisee. While I cannot speak to Moshe's perspective on God's grace, I know that in my own life I have struggled with a belief that reduces my relationship with God to a simple mathematical equation that divine favor results from doing what is right. I believe that God blesses correct choices, but my fundamental standing before a holy God is not dependent upon my good behavior. I have failed to meet God's standards (Romans 3:10).[1]

1. Romans 3:10—"as it is written, 'There is none righteous, not even one.'"

Paul indicated in Galatians 2:16–21[2] that keeping a series of commandments could not produce a righteous standing before God, but that a correct position is linked to faith, grace, and Jesus' death. These three things are key.

Reflection Questions

1. How would you define a "good" person and how does it apply to you?

2. Is a person's goodness enough to meet divine standards of moral excellence?

3. If a right standing before God is not dependent upon good deeds, what is the motivation for zealously doing them?

---

2. Galatians 2:16–21—"nevertheless knowing that a man is not justified by the works of the Law but through faith in Christ Jesus, even we have believed in Christ Jesus, that we may be justified by faith in Christ, and not by the works of the Law; since by the works of the Law shall no flesh be justified. But if, while seeking to be justified in Christ, we ourselves have also been found sinners, is Christ then a minister of sin? May it never be! For if I rebuild what I have *once* destroyed, I prove myself to be a transgressor. For through the Law, I died to the Law, that I might live to God. I have been crucified with Christ; and it is no longer I who live, but Christ lives in me; and the *life* which I now live in the flesh I live by faith in the Son of God, who loved me, and delivered Himself up for me. I do not nullify the grace of God; for if righteousness *comes* through the Law, then Christ died needlessly."

13

No Condemnation for Christ Followers

There is therefore now no condemnation for those who are in Christ Jesus. For the law of the Spirit of life in Christ Jesus has set you free from the law of sin and of death. For what the Law could not do, weak as it was through the flesh, God *did*: sending His own Son in the likeness of sinful flesh and *as an offering* for sin, He condemned sin in the flesh, in order that the requirement of the Law might be fulfilled in us, who do not walk according to the flesh, but according to the Spirit.

—ROMANS 8:1–4

One of my greatest struggles is over self-condemnation. Most of the time that I am wronged, I am rather quick to forgive and to move forward. The bigger the hurt, the harder it is to let go; but I am generally in a positive place from the standpoint of forgiveness, that is, in terms of forgiving others. *Forgiving myself is another matter.* I am overly guilty by disposition and apologize much too often and about things that I should not. At times, it is not easy to be around me. More than one person has told me to stop saying sorry so much. My over-apologizing carries over into the spiritual realm in terms of asking God for forgiveness for things that are unnecessary. At times, I also apologize about the same thing more than once—this is true when I interact with humans, too. The root issue is that I am very sensitive in seeking to be right with people and with God, which on the whole is a good thing, but it often goes too far. Repetitive apologizing stems from a basic flaw: I do not accept the forgiveness of God and others as genuine. I continue to carry the guilt and condemnation even when I have been released from such burdens by the ones I wronged. I condemn myself when there is no condemnation. I have much to learn from Romans 8.

Condemnation (*katakrima*) is an act of judgment in which the one judging recognizes that a person has transgressed a moral standard and is, therefore, worthy of punishment.[xvii] Humans can condemn humans (Luke 11:32),[1] which means that the condemnation is not always justified, as in Jesus' case when the authorities believed that he was worthy of execution (Mark 14:64).[2] God can condemn humanity (1 Corinthians 11:32)[3] and has already done so to iniquity (Romans 8:3).[4] Romans 8:1 explains that condemnation does not exist for the ones in Jesus. It is not that Jesus' followers merit such an exemption based upon their own actions; instead, their standing before God is based upon the actions of Jesus, resulting in a correct or justified status that is able to withstand any charge (Romans 8:28–34).[5]

1. Luke 11:32—"The men of Nineveh shall stand up with this generation at the judgment and condemn it, because they repented at the preaching of Jonah; and behold, something greater than Jonah is here."

2. Mark 14:64—"'You have heard the blasphemy; how does it seem to you?' And they all condemned Him to be deserving of death."

3. 1 Corinthians 11:32—"But when we are judged, we are disciplined by the Lord in order that we may not be condemned along with the world."

4. Rom 8:3—"For what the Law could not do, weak as it was through the flesh, God *did*: sending His own Son in the likeness of sinful flesh and *as an offering* for sin, He condemned sin in the flesh."

5. Romans 8:28–34—"And we know that God causes all things to work together for good to those who love God, to those who are called according to *His* purpose. For whom He foreknew, He also predestined *to become* conformed to the image of His Son, that He might be the firstborn among many brethren; and whom He predestined, these He also called; and whom He called, these He also justified; and whom he justified, these He also glorified. What then shall we say to these things? If God *is* for us, who *is* against us? He who did not spare His own Son, but delivered Him up for us all, how will He not also with Him freely give us all things? Who will bring a charge against God's elect? God

There is an example of condemnation and release from it that is worthy of reflection. The account is found in John 8 and represents the testing of Jesus by the religious establishment of his day. A woman was brought forward while Jesus was teaching at the Temple in Jerusalem. She was rightly condemned to death according to the Law because she was discovered in the midst of an adulterous act. People wanted to know how Jesus would respond. Beyond writing on the ground, his response was that the person who was free from sin should initiate the stoning process. This prompted everyone to leave for they recognized that they, too, had transgressed God's moral standards in some way. None of the accusers remained to condemn her. In his dialogue with her, Jesus proclaimed: "Neither do I condemn you; go your way. From now on sin no more" (John 8:11).

This narrative embodies the notion of how a person in Jesus is free from condemnation. The Christ-follower has sinned and deserves punishment. Yet, the judgement and the penalty are not placed upon the individual's shoulders. Mercy and grace are the driving forces behind such deliverance. Thank God that he has a ready supply of both!

Reflection Questions

1. How deserving of condemnation are we?

2. Why do we not stand condemned in front of a holy God?

3. In what ways do you struggle with self-condemnation like me and how should we respond in the face of it?

---

is the one who justifies; who is the one who condemns? Christ Jesus is He who died, yes, rather who was raised, who is at the right hand of God, who also intercedes for us."

I 4

Condemnation of Sin

There is therefore now no condemnation for those who are in Christ
Jesus. For the law of the Spirit of life in Christ Jesus has set you free
from the law of sin and of death. For what the Law could not do,
weak as it was through the flesh, God *did*: sending His own Son in
the likeness of sinful flesh and *as an offering* for sin, He condemned
sin in the flesh, in order that the requirement of the Law might be
fulfilled in us, who do not walk according to the flesh, but according
to the Spirit.

—ROMANS 8:1–4

Prior to the verses represented here, Romans 7 addresses the
power that sin holds over the human body. The power is so
strong that Paul declared that within him there was a conflict between two opposing forces. The result was that he found himself
doing the exact opposite of what he wanted to accomplish. The
culprit was sin working through his flesh. His mind aligned with
God's law, but his body served sin's law. Following this discussion
of the tug-a-war of the flesh versus the mind, Romans 8 begins
with the declaration that condemnation does not exist for the
follower of Jesus and that "the law of the Spirit of life in Christ
Jesus" (8:2) secured freedom from the law associated with death
and iniquity. The passage continues by indicating that the Law was

unable to accomplish the defeat of sin; rather, victory was won by divine action. It was necessary for God to step into the situation. God condemned iniquity through the process of the Father's sending of Jesus in human likeness to serve as a sin-offering. The NASB presents words in italics when the words are not literally in the original language. Thus, the Greek behind what is translated in Romans 8:3 as "*as an offering* for sin" only reads "for sin" (*peri hamartias*)[xviii] in the original language. Still "sin-sacrifice" or "sin-offering" is an acceptable rendering of the phrase "for sin." The same terminology is found in the biblical quotation of Psalm 40:6[xix] in Hebrews 10:6[1] and the Greek version of Leviticus 16:3[2] to indicate that "for sin" can designate a type of sacrifice, that is, a sacrifice to deal with sin.[xx] Regardless of the translation ("for sin" or "for a sin-sacrifice"), the appearance of Jesus in the world is presented here as instrumental in the process of sin's condemnation. God's judgement was directed at sin instead of those who follow Jesus.

As Romans 8 continues, more information is provided concerning the contrast between the physical body and the spiritual realm, providing practical advice on the way to wage war against the sinful nature. Sin has been defeated through the work of Jesus (8:3) and now we must endeavor to slay the works of the flesh through the help of God's Spirit (8:12-14).[3] Galatians 5:16-24[4]

1. Hebrews 10:6—"In whole burnt offerings and *sacrifices* for sin thou hast taken no pleasure."

2. Leviticus 16:3—"Aaron shall enter the holy place with this: with a bull for a sin offering and a ram for a burnt offering."

3. Romans 8:12-14—"So then, brethren, we are under obligation, not to the flesh, to live according to the flesh—for if you are living according to the flesh, you must die; but if by the Spirit you are putting to death the deeds of the body, you will live. For all who are being led by the Spirit of God, these are sons of God."

4. Galatians 5:16-24—"But I say, walk by the Spirit, and you will not carry out the desire of the flesh. For the flesh sets its desire against the Spirit, and the Spirit against the flesh; for these are in opposition to one another, so that you may not do the things that you please. But if you are led by the Spirit, you are not under the Law. Now the deeds of the flesh are evident, which are: immorality, impurity, sensuality, idolatry, sorcery, enmities, strife, jealousy, outbursts

presents the differing results of walking by the flesh rather than by the Spirit. The differences are great. The ultimate victory in the war over sin has been accomplished, but the daily battles constantly occur at the personal level. The battles are ever present! Even in seeking to write this paragraph I had to deal with a situation in which I was faced with a choice to walk according to heavenly ways or by earthly means. I did not make the choice consciously, all too easily slipping into my natural tendencies and allowing myself to get frustrated to the point of sin. Among the many biblical principles related to how a person can better make the correct choice in the midst of battle, Romans 8 signifies the importance of a mind that is focused upon spiritual affairs, or more specifically upon the Holy Spirit, who indwells the believer.[xxi] One of the useful techniques that I have found to focus the mind in the right direction is to memorize Scripture. I became lazy in this area and out of habit (recall my Awana days?) until a good friend of mine, Mike Frazier, encouraged me to learn relatively lengthy portions of the Bible. Saturating my thoughts with words like those from 1 Corinthians 13 about the kindness and patience of love has helped me, through the guidance of the Holy Spirit, to choose the righteous path and to avoid sinning in the form of being too upset. Unfortunately, those words escaped my mind while constructing this study. Of course, Romans 8 tells us that nothing is wasted: God turns all things into positives (8:28).[5] My misstep, for instance, helped me better appreciate the portion of Scripture under consideration, and that is certainly a good result.

---

of anger, disputes, dissensions, factions, envying, drunkenness, carousing, and things like these, of which I forewarn you just as I have forewarned you that those who practice such things shall not inherit the kingdom of God. But the fruit of the Spirit is love, joy, peace, patience, kindness, goodness, faithfulness, gentleness, self-control; against such things there is no law. Now those who belong to Christ Jesus have crucified the flesh with its passions and desires."

5. Romans 8:28—"And we know that God causes all things to work together for good to those who love God, to those who are called according to *His* purpose."

Reflection Questions

1. How would you describe your inner war between choosing God's path and the ways of the flesh?

2. What does Romans 8 tell us about what side won the ultimate victory and how was it achieved?

3. How can we better apply that victory in our lives when dealing with fleshly tendencies?

15

A Sacrificed Intercessor

And we know that God causes all things to work together for good
to those who love God, to those who are called according to *His*
purpose. For whom He foreknew, He also predestined *to become*
conformed to the image of His Son, that He might be the firstborn
among many brethren; and whom He predestined, these He also
called; and whom He called, these He also justified; and whom he
justified, these He also glorified. What then shall we say to these
things? If God *is* for us, who *is* against us? He who did not spare His
own Son, but delivered Him up for us all, how will He not also with
Him freely give us all things? Who will bring a charge against God's
elect? God is the one who justifies; who is the one who condemns?
Christ Jesus is He who died, yes, rather who was raised, who is at the
right hand of God, who also intercedes for us.

—ROMANS 8:28–34

We see here a similar sacrificial reference to the death of Jesus
as found in Galatians 2:20,[1] but with a different emphasis on
the actor. In the verse from Galatians, Jesus is noted as sacrificially

---

1. Galatians 2:20—"I have been crucified with Christ; and it is no longer I
who live, but Christ lives in me; and the *life* which I now live in the flesh I live
by faith in the Son of God, who loved me, and delivered Himself up for me."

giving over or delivering himself, whereas Romans 8:32 presents the Father as the actor in the sacrifice. Romans 8 also provides a parallel between God the Father and Abraham by indicating that the son was not spared (see Genesis 22:12). The above translation of Romans 8:32 could be modified to read: "How will the one who did not even spare his own son, but sacrificially gave him over (*paradidōmi*) on behalf of us all, not also with him forgive us from all things?" Both the idea of forgiving or freely giving are viable translations of the final part of the verse, but forgiveness fits the context better from the standpoint of condemnation or, rather, a lack thereof for the Christian.[xxii]

Earlier in Romans and in another of Paul's treatments of Abraham's righteous faith, reference is made to Jesus being sacrificially given over (*paradidōmi*) due to sin, apparently by the Father. More specifically, the passage states: "but for our sake also, to whom it will be reckoned, as those who believe in Him who raised Jesus our Lord from the dead, *He* who was delivered up because of our transgressions, and was raised because of our justification" (Romans 4:24–25). Here we see the importance of belief in relation to righteousness, the reason behind Jesus' sacrifice (due to sin), and the role played by Jesus' resurrection (for justification).

In returning to Romans 8:31–34, we can see some overlapping ideas in Romans 4 and 8. Chapter 8 deals with justification (being in a right standing) as if one were in a religiously-oriented court of law. You may immediately think of our discussion about 1 John 2 (above, chapter 5). In the Romans 8 passage under consideration, it represents a scenario in which charges against and condemnations of Christians could not be leveled. I get the sense that Paul's meaning is that anyone who levels such accusations would have to contend with the judge, who is the Father, and go up against Jesus, who acts as intercessor for his followers. Jesus' role as intercessor in response to condemnation is similar to 1 John 2 with its representation of Jesus' activity as an advocate to stand up for the legally correct status of the Christian.[xxiii] There is also in Romans 8 the concept of the intercessory activity of the Holy Spirit (8:26).[2]

2. Romans 8:26—"And in the same way the Spirit also helps our weakness;

Human weakness, the text indicates, limits the ability of humans to pray adequately, but the Holy Spirit makes up for the deficiency by interceding with groans that cannot be expressed with words.

Reflection Questions

1. When have you found yourself at a loss for words in prayer? Was it due to feelings of frustration, inadequacy, ignorance, or something else? How common do you think others feel at a loss for words?

2. What types of intercessory activities are represented in Romans 8:26–39?

3. How do the intercessory roles found in the passage provide you with encouragement or relief?

---

for we do not know how to pray as we should, but the Spirit Himself intercedes for *us* with groanings too deep for words."

16

Justification vs. Condemnation

But the free gift is not like the transgression. For if by the transgression of the one the many died, much more did the grace of God and the gift by the grace of the one Man, Jesus Christ, abound to the many. And the gift is not like *that which came* through the one who sinned; for on the one hand the judgment *arose* from one *transgression* resulting in condemnation, but on the other hand the free gift *arose* from many transgressions resulting in justification. For if by the transgression of the one, death reigned through the one, much more those who receive the abundance of grace and of the gift of righteousness will reign in life through the One, Jesus Christ. So then as through one transgression there resulted condemnation to all men, even so through one act of righteousness there resulted justification of life to all men. For as through the one man's disobedience the many were made sinners, even so through the obedience of the One the many will be made righteous.

—ROMANS 5:15-19

Romans 5:16 and 18 are the only other verses in the New Testament that use the same word for condemnation (*katakrima*) that is found in Romans 8:1.[1] Romans 5 is an important passage

1. Romans 8:1—"There is therefore now no condemnation for those who

48

that has an overall focus upon justification. It explains that justification is founded upon the death of Jesus and that it is applied to the Christ-follower through faith. What, then, is justification and why must it be established? Based solely upon the way the concept is presented in Romans 5:16 and 18, one could simply state that justification is the direct opposite of condemnation. In that sense, the idea is related to innocence and the lack of punishment. While this is true, the sense of the word is more complicated. Even in the translation provided above for Romans 5:16 and 18, the translators chose to render one of the words related to justification in two differing ways: "justification" and "act of righteousness."[xxiv] "Justification" is not a particularly common word in the New Testament.[xxv] The verbal idea of justifying (*dikaioō*) is more common; for example, Romans 5:1 (see 5:9) reads: "Therefore having been justified by faith, we have peace with God through our Lord Jesus Christ." The verb (*dikaioō*) appears in the Bible (both in the Greek version of the Hebrew Bible and New Testament) to indicate such ideas as declaring righteous, acquitting, and securing vindication.[xxvi] When considering how the verbal idea is presented in passages like Romans 4[2] and Galatians 3,[3] one gets the sense that at the heart of being justified is the recognition of personal righteousness in God's eyes. It is a status given to the individual based upon faith in which the person is regarded as *morally and judicially upright*.[xxvii] This status means that the person is not condemned. Faith, a justified status, and freedom from condemnation are at the heart of Romans 5.[xxviii]

---

are in Christ Jesus."

2. Romans 4:2–5—"For if Abraham was justified by works, he has something to boast about; but not before God. For what does the Scripture say? 'And Abraham believed God, and it was reckoned to him as righteousness.' Now to the one who works, his wage is not reckoned as a favor, but as what is due. But to the one who does not work, but believes in Him who justifies the ungodly, his faith is reckoned as righteousness."

3. Galatians 3:6–8—"Even so Abraham believed God, and it was reckoned to him as righteousness. Therefore, be sure that it is those who are of faith who are sons of Abraham. And the Scripture, foreseeing that God would justify the Gentiles by faith, preached the gospel beforehand to Abraham, *saying*, 'All the nations shall be blessed in you.'"

There is more to the story, however, in terms of the process by which the upright status is provided. Romans 3 indicates that no person is righteous enough on their own merit. In Romans 5, the root of the problem is explained as Adam's disobedience (see v. 14).[4] The Christian understanding of how sin spread to all people is provided in Romans 5. It draws upon the Genesis account of Adam and Eve's disobedience in eating of the forbidden fruit and their expulsion from the Garden of Eden. Cut off from the garden's Tree of Life, living continuously was no longer possible for them. Romans 5 indicates that death and sin became the norm for humanity. By contrast, a single act of sacrificial obedience dramatically altered the course of human history, leading to justification instead of condemnation.

Reflection Questions

1. How would you define justification based upon Romans 5?

2. How can the concept of justification assist us when faced by feelings of condemnation?

3. What is the ultimate result of justification as mentioned at the end of Romans 5?

4. Romans 5:14—"Nevertheless death reigned from Adam until Moses, even over those who had not sinned in the likeness of the offense of Adam, who is a type of Him who was to come."

17

Sacrificially Giving, Transgressions, and Securing Justification

Now not for his sake only was it written, that it was reckoned to him, but for our sake also, to whom it will be reckoned, as those who believe in Him who raised Jesus our Lord from the dead, *He* who was delivered up because of our transgressions, and was raised because of our justification. Therefore having been justified by faith, we have peace with God through our Lord Jesus Christ . . . For while we were still helpless, at the right time Christ died for the ungodly. For one will hardly die for a righteous man; though perhaps for the good man someone would dare even to die. But God demonstrates His own love toward us, in that while we were yet sinners, Christ died for us. Much more then, having now been justified by His blood, we shall be saved from the wrath *of God* through Him.

—ROMANS 4:23—5:1, 6-9

The sacrificial nature of Jesus' death is explained from the end of Romans 4 through Romans 5 in two fundamental ways. First, there is the reference to the sacrificial giving over (*paradidōmi*) of Jesus (4:25), or at least that he was given over due to people's sins. The verb can also mean giving over in an act of betrayal (John

18:2)[1] and verse 25 does not designate the actor behind the giving, be it the Father, Jesus, or even Judas. The context would seem to imply that the Father was the actor, but the verse is ambiguous. Pauline literature uses the verb in a sacrificial sense several times, including in a passage already studied (Romans 8:32)[2] and in others we will encounter below (Ephesians 5:2 and 25).[3] In Romans 4:25, the focus of the process of giving over is described as a result of iniquity, which further supports a sacrificial interpretation of the verse. A sacrificial sense is clear, moreover, in light of Romans 5. There the discussion of Jesus' death for sinners continues and links the process of justification to his blood. The linkage between dying for sin and the effects of the sacrificial victim's blood was not written coincidentally.

Blood was instrumental in the cleansing process in the context of Israel's sacrificial system. The Bible is filled with references to rituals using blood, e.g., sin-offerings in Leviticus 4. We will see in the days ahead that New Testament writers drew upon such rites to describe the functional nature of Jesus' death. Romans 5:9 indicates that his blood was spilled in a sacrificial act that resulted in bringing about a justified (or righteous) standing before God with the result that salvation from future wrath was secured. The wrath explained in Romans 5 is punitive divine anger resulting from moral transgressions. In the religious system of Israel, when commandments were not kept, divine anger and punishment could follow (Deuteronomy 28-30). Slaying animals in sacrifice and ritually using their blood would produce cleansing and the restoration of a correct relationship between God and his people (Leviticus 16). Romans 5 explains that the correct standing (justification) with God results in a peaceful relationship in which there

1. John 18:2—"Now Judas also, who was betraying Him, knew the place; for Jesus had often met there with His disciples."

2. Romans 8:32—"He who did not spare His own Son, but delivered Him up for us all, how will He not also with Him freely give us all things?"

3. Ephesians 5:2 and 25—"and walk in love, just as Christ also loved you, and gave Himself up for us, an offering and a sacrifice to God as a fragrant aroma . . . Husbands, love your wives, just as Christ also loved the church and gave Himself up for her."

was a movement of Jesus' followers from the position of enemies to one of reconciliation. According to Colossians 1:20–22[4] and Ephesians 2:13–16,[5] Jesus' blood and flesh were significant in the reconciliation. Both the reconciliation between Jews and Gentiles that Jesus facilitated and the reconciliation of people to the Father are addressed in Ephesians 2.

Reflection Questions

1. Read over Romans 5:6–9 and consider the contrast that is being offered between a person's potential willingness to die for a righteous person and Christ's death for unrighteous sinners. What does that say about divine love?

2. Why was there a need for reconciliation between humans and God?

3. How often do you feel at peace with God and should you have a more conscious recognition of it?

4. Colossians 1:20–22—"and through Him to reconcile all things to Himself, having made peace through the blood of His cross; through Him, *I say*, whether things on earth or things in heaven. And although you were formerly alienated and hostile in mind, *engaged* in evil deeds, yet He has now reconciled you in His fleshly body through death, in order to present you before Him holy and blameless and beyond reproach."

5. Ephesians 2:13–16—"But now in Christ Jesus you who formerly were far off have been brought near by the blood of Christ. For He Himself is our peace, who made both *groups into* one, and broke down the barrier of the dividing wall, by abolishing in His flesh the enmity, *which is* the Law of commandments *contained* in ordinances, that in Himself He might make the two into one new man, *thus* establishing peace, and might reconcile them both in one body to God though the cross, by it having put to death the enmity."

18

Moving Forward, but Faltering

But if, while seeking to be justified in Christ, we ourselves have also
been found sinners, is Christ then a minister of sin? May it never
be! For if I rebuild what I have *once* destroyed, I prove myself to be a
transgressor. For through the Law, I died to the Law, that I might live
to God. I have been crucified with Christ; and it is no longer I who
live, but Christ lives in me; and the *life* which I now live in the flesh I
live by faith in the Son of God, who loved me, and delivered Himself
up for me. I do not nullify the grace of God; for if righteousness
comes through the Law, then Christ died needlessly.

—GALATIANS 2:17–21

In today's passage, Paul was considering what happens when
people seek out justification, but fall into sin.[xxix] Galatians 2
contrasts the possible benefits of the Law, which does not justify,
to faith in Jesus, which does result in justification. Faith, in short,
results in gaining a righteous status (see Galatians 3, too).[xxx] There
is also an important focus here upon grace and the sacrificial death
of Jesus, both of which are key elements in securing an upright
standing before God. The teaching regarding the identification of
the believer with Christ's crucifixion is significant as well. I will
address that topic later.

When thinking about this passage, I was reminded of a song by DC Talk, a popular Christian group that has since disbanded. In "What if I stumble?" from the album *Jesus Freak* (1995), the group considered the ramifications of making a mistake that would reflect poorly on the Christian faith. Such a concern is legitimate given the realities of life and the human propensity to fail morally. In Galatians 2, Paul addressed similar concepts: What if we misstep in our pursuit of holiness and how does that reflect upon Christ? Rather than focus on Jesus, DC Talk was concerned about how shortcomings would make other Christians look foolish, apparently both the fellow band members and Christians in general. Paul argued that when Christians sin, it does not mean that Jesus is "a minister of sin." The word translated as minister (*diakonos*) can indicate the position of servant; elsewhere, the NASB translates the word in relation to being a servant to God (2 Corinthians 6:4)[1] or others (Mark 10:43).[2] When we sin, does that designate Jesus as one who serves sin or promotes a path of wrongful moral action? Paul explained that it is not Jesus who is to blame for moral errors, but the individual—in this case, Paul himself.

I have actually found comfort in the way that Paul wrote about sin in this passage because it mentions the rebuilding of sin in one's life when it was previously destroyed. It might sound strange to you that I have found solace in the text, but it is for the following reason: in my pursuit of life with God, I have found victory by God's grace and empowerment over certain wrongful behaviors. I have also experienced moments of defeat, falling into old patterns. One of the potential reasons for this is that I let my guard down. Destroying sinful habits or slaying fleshly works requires offensive action through God's help. As previously noted, the ultimate victory over sin was accomplished through Jesus' sacrificial death, but life in the flesh continues to necessitate battle. When a particular offensive is over and we think that a specific behavior is

1. 2 Corinthians 6:4—"but in everything commending ourselves as servants of God, in much endurance, in afflictions, in hardships, in distresses."

2. Mark 10:43—"But it is not so among you, but whoever wishes to become great among you shall be your servant."

conquered, we can become passive and unmindful of the need to build up our defenses. Left unguarded, we are susceptible to the rebuilding of sinful works in our lives. The greater the destroyed work, the greater the probability that it will be rebuilt. I am not promoting some sort of defeatism in which I am claiming that a sinful behavior cannot be eradicated completely from a person's life. I believe that through the power of Jesus' atoning work and the Holy Spirit that such a triumph can be experienced. Yet, I recognize in my own life that I can fall into old behaviors. Paul's perspective is that such failure is not Christ's fault, but our own—this is a pretty obvious concept, though God does get blamed for a lot of stuff. Paul also explained that we are living a new life in Christ by means of faith. It is through this faith that battles are won and grace is experienced. It is fitting that grace is mentioned at the end of a passage dealing with moral failure. Elsewhere Paul explained that grace multiplied in the face of sin's increase (Romans 5:20).[3] When we transgress, including in areas that we once overcame, divine favor abounds leading to forgiveness and renewal.

Reflection Questions

1. To what extent do you find comfort in Galatians 2:17–21?

2. What areas in your life require consistent vigilance and prayer lest sinful practices are rebuilt?

3. Elsewhere Paul wrote that we are to be above reproach as examples in this world (Philippians 2:15). Have you encountered criticism of Christ when moral failure occurs within the church, and are such denunciations focused upon the right one according to Galatians 2? Who is to blame?

---

3. Romans 5:20—"And the Law came in that the transgression might increase; but where sin increased, grace abounded all the more."

19

Following the Example of Sacrificial Giving

And be kind to one another, tender-hearted, forgiving each other, just as God in Christ also has forgiven you. Therefore be imitators of God, as beloved children; and walk in love, just as Christ also loved you, and gave Himself up for us, an offering and a sacrifice to God as a fragrant aroma.

—EPHESIANS 4:32–5:2

This passage provides the strongest evidence so far encountered that the concept of giving oneself or another person over can be regarded sacrificially, because the relevant verb, translated as "gave up" (*paradidōmi*), that we have met in several studies thus far is modified here by such words as "offering" (*prosphora*), "sacrifice" (*thusia*), and "fragrant aroma" (*osmē + euōdia*). The first two are self-explanatory: Jesus' act of giving himself over is equated to presenting to God a sacrifice and an offering. The idea of it being an aroma corresponds to the manner in which the Hebrew Bible speaks about the satisfying or calming smell of burnt-sacrifice as it wafts up into the heavens and reaches God to provoke a positive response (Genesis 8:21). Jesus' sacrificial death produced such a reaction in the Father.

Both in this study and the next, the self-sacrificial giving over of Jesus is brought forth in the midst of discussions about interpersonal relationships to explain that such interactions should be modeled on the self-sacrifice of Christ. Please observe that Ephesians 4:32 and 5:1-2 are connected even though they appear in two different chapters in our Bibles. "Therefore" is a transitional statement to indicate that just as God acted towards the church at Ephesus, they should mimic the divine example in their interactions with each other like children who repeat the behaviors of their parents. This is a tall order, particularly in light of how the text continues. The believers were to have a life characterized by the type of love seen in Jesus, who took love to its farthest extreme of self-sacrifice. Much of what we learn comes by example. We also come by some things naturally. We will not develop pure selfless love when left to our own devices, however. Indeed, we already spoke about the biblical perspective that our love stems from God loving us first. Our human tendencies move us in the direction of self-love or selfishness. Doing the things that we want or feel like doing regardless of how it affects others gets to the heart of many of our interpersonal problems. Many of our hurtful behaviors stem from circumstances in which we are paying too much attention to self-interest. To be like Christ, we must deny ourselves to the point of carrying the implements of our own destructions (crosses), just as he taught (Matthew 16:24).[1] In Ephesians 5, we see that we should love others to the point of self-sacrifice. Just to be clear: the emphasis is upon figurative self-sacrifice, not literal sacrificial death.[xxxi]

As we think about these things, I wish to provide a few warnings. First, we must be careful that we are sacrificially giving ourselves in the proper ways. We cannot do everything that people ask of us. There are times when we need to say "no" and there are things that people should do for themselves. We must prayerfully consider how to respond. I, all too often, have agreed to do things to my personal detriment—unfortunately, I am an avid people-pleaser. Second, we must not get too caught up in sacrificially serving others that we miss out on meaningful times of

---

1. Matthew 16:24—"Then Jesus said to His disciples, 'If anyone wishes to come after Me, let him deny himself, and take up his cross, and follow Me.'"

interpersonal interactions. I realized last night, for example, that I have a tendency to act like Martha (doing things for people) that I neglect quality time with those who are important in my life. Mary had it figured out (see Luke 10:38–42).[2]

We must sacrificially love others while avoiding the Martha-syndrome of doing good things at the wrong times.

Reflection Questions

1. To what extent do you feel that you are following Jesus' example of sacrificial love in the ways you interact with others?

2. Are there particular people for whom you are lacking love and how will today's Scripture help you in that relationship?

3. Do you find yourself agreeing to too many good things at the expense of others in your life? How does the story of Martha and Mary encourage you to slow down and establish times for quality interaction? What practical steps can you take today to make a change?

---

2. Luke 10:38–42—"Now as they were traveling along, He entered a certain village; and a woman named Martha welcomed Him into her home. And she had a sister called Mary, who moreover was listening to the Lord's word, seated at His feet. But Martha was distracted with all her preparations; and she came up *to Him*, and said, 'Lord, do You not care that my sister has left me to do all the serving alone? Then tell her to help me.' But the Lord answered and said to her, 'Martha, Martha, you are worried and bothered about so many things; but *only* a few things are necessary, really *only* one, for Mary has chosen the good part, which shall not be taken away from her.'"

20

Following the Example of Sacrificial Giving (Again)

Husbands, love your wives, just as Christ also loved the church and gave Himself up for her; that He might sanctify her, having cleansed her by the washing of water with the word, that He might present to Himself the church in all her glory, having no spot or wrinkle or any such thing; but that she should be holy and blameless. So husbands ought also to love their own wives as their own bodies. He who loves his own wife loves himself.

—EPHESIANS 5:25-28

We were married young by today's standards. I was 19 and Krista was 21. At that age, I was old enough to get married, but too young to book a hotel room in my name—a strange experience for a man trying to arrange his honeymoon! It is good that we did not require a rental car because I was probably too young for that as well. Despite some planning issues and the fact that the surprise destination was inadvertently leaked to Krista, we had a terrific trip. Krista graciously did not tell me that the surprise was ruined until long after the honeymoon. By the time she found out, it was too late to change destinations; besides, I would not have been able to book the rooms in any case! At the time

I started writing this study, we were around three months away from celebrating our twenty-first wedding anniversary. Krista is a great wife. She sacrificially loves me, our sons, and others. She is a Spirit-filled woman who loves God and eagerly seeks to infuse Christ into our household. While Ephesians 5:25 can encourage sacrificial love among both spouses, it is focused on husbands. It specifically speaks to me—but even if you are not married, the idea of sacrificially loving someone in your life is an important principle.

The model for behavior is to love my wife in the same manner that Jesus expressed his love for the church body, which, as noted previously, went so far as to give himself totally over to a sacrificial death. In case you were wondering, the same verb in Ephesians 5:2 is used in 5:25 to denote a sacrificial death.

Yesterday, we noticed how sacrificial love was mandated for the believers. What does today's passage mean for husbands and for me, in particular? In the past 20+ years, I have not at any point suffered flogging and execution on her behalf, and I certainly have not carried her sins upon my shoulders. Jesus did all of that and more for our wives. There may be a time where God calls us to give our lives in defense of our spouses and to do so would be the greatest act of love that we could offer. More practically, this verse tells us to give ourselves sacrificially in a figurative sense by denying our needs and desires for the benefit of our wives. We must model Christ's love in our ever interaction. It might sound trivial and I do not wish to diminish what Christ did, but the sacrificial giving of ourselves in the context of marriage may mean taking care of aspects of the daily grind with a generous and loving attitude. I have even thought of this passage when doing the dishes—again it sounds diminutive (and it is in comparison to Jesus' work), but being sacrificial requires the right response in terms of the big acts of giving, such as literally dying to defend a spouse, to the small acts of giving, like getting up at 5:40 am with an early rising child so that a spouse can sleep longer. Admittedly, I do a lot of little things for my wife, but I do not often have a sacrificial attitude. I am still developing.

Sacrificial loving does not mean that a person becomes robot-like, catering to every wish, whim, and desire of a spouse; rather, like Christ, a husband must submit his will to that of the Father's. As the Father leads us to act sacrificially, then we must do so.

Reflection Questions

1. What does it mean to love as Christ did?

2. How should such love be manifested in your relationship with your spouse?

3. If you are not married, how does this passage encourage you to live towards others in your family or close circle of friends?

21

Sanctifying Blood

We have an altar, from which those who serve the tabernacle have no right to eat. For the bodies of those animals whose blood is brought into the holy place by the high priest *as an offering* for sin, are burned outside the camp. Therefore Jesus also, that He might sanctify the people through His own blood, suffered outside the gate. Hence, let us go out to Him outside the camp, bearing His reproach. For here we do not have a lasting city, but we are seeking *the city* which is to come. Through Him then, let us continually offer up a sacrifice of praise to God, that is, the fruit of lips that give thanks to His name. And do not neglect doing good and sharing; for with such sacrifices God is pleased.

—HEBREWS 13:10‑16

T he book of Hebrews is particularly rich in the ways that it addresses the topic of the sacrificial death of Jesus. The work is detailed in its engagement with the Jewish sacrificial system in order to demonstrate not simply the parallels between Jesus and that system, but to represent Christ as doing something greater than the earthly order with its blood sacrifices and sacred priesthood. In the passage before us, we find ourselves at the end of the book in a portion that returns to the sacrificial death of Jesus and moves into a call for the followers of Christ to participate in his suffering and to present sacrifices to God through Jesus, their high priest.

The material covered in this section of Hebrews 13 and elsewhere in Hebrews requires more than a single day of reflection. We will first consider the topic of sanctification, which was already brought forth in yesterday's text when Ephesians 5:26[1] indicated that one of the purposes behind Jesus' sacrificial death was the sanctification of the church.

The spilling of Jesus' blood—the very essence of his life—is described as having a sanctifying function in Hebrews 13. The ritual parallelism in the passage is the Jewish Day of Atonement or Yom Kippur, which is described in Leviticus 16. The Day of Atonement was the one time of the year at which point the high priest was allowed access into the holiest part of the Temple or Tabernacle to apply blood upon the mercy seat of the Ark of the Covenant. The day was about covering the sins of the entire community. Hebrews deals with this topic elsewhere and we shall return to it. Today I wish to focus on the sanctifying power of blood. The high priest and his fellow priests, for example, could not serve at the sanctuary unless they were consecrated or sanctified through the use of animal blood. They also had to wear sanctified clothing (see Exodus 28–29). The same word for sanctifying (*hagiazō*) the priests and their clothing in Exodus 29:21[2] is used in Hebrews 13 concerning the purpose of Jesus' suffering. Jesus died to make people holy by means of his blood. The word appears in other parts of Hebrews, such as in Hebrews 9:13–14, which contrasts the sanctifying power of animals to the cleansing effects of Jesus' blood: "For if the blood of goats and bulls and the ashes of a heifer sprinkling those who have been defiled, sanctify for the cleansing of the flesh, how much more will the blood of Christ, who through the eternal Spirit

1. Ephesians 5:26—"that He might sanctify her, having cleansed her by the washing of water with the word."

2. Exodus 29:21—"Then you shall take some of the blood that is on the altar and some of the anointing oil, and sprinkle *it* on Aaron and on his garments, and on his sons and on his sons' garments with him; so he and his garments shall be consecrated, as well as his sons and his sons' garments with him."

offered Himself without blemish to God, cleanse your conscience from dead works to serve the living God?" Cleansing is part of the process of sanctification, but sanctification is more specifically an act of *consecration* or *making something holy.*[xxxii]

The sacrificial death of Jesus, unlike animal sacrifice, was effective for all time and does not require repetition for the removal of sin. Yet, sanctification is presented in Hebrews as both a completed and an ongoing matter in the life of the Christ-follower. This two-fold aspect of sanctification can be seen in the different verbal forms used in Hebrews 10:10 and 10:14. The ESV translation captures the difference nicely: "And by that will we *have been sanctified* through the offering of the body of Jesus Christ once for all . . . For by a single offering he has perfected for all time those who *are being sanctified*" (emphasis added).[xxxiii] Regarding the idea of perfection, the context suggests that the perfection is in terms of the complete forgiveness of sin, not perfection in the sense that members of the church will never sin again. This makes sense in light of a later chapter in Hebrews, which encourages Christians to lay aside sinful habits (12:1)[3] and specifies that God disciplines his children so that they can participate in his holiness (12:10).[4] That chapter also encourages people to seek sanctification (12:14).[5]

We should be in the process of becoming holier in the way that we live. Sanctification is an ongoing process in our lives, but we still have a consecrated status before God due to the sacrifice of Jesus. This holy status reflects the idea of a completed sanctification, which is provided to us at the point of conversion. This status is reflected in the term "saint" or "holy individual" (*hagios*), which is what Christians are called in the New Testament.[xxxiv] 1 Corinthians 1:2 puts the ideas of sanctification and the saintly or holy designation for Christians together nicely when it states: "to

3. Hebrews 12:1—"Therefore, since we have so great a cloud of witnesses surrounding us, let us also lay aside every encumbrance, and the sin which so easily entangles us, and let us run with endurance the race that is set before us."

4. Hebrews 12:10—"For they disciplined us for a short time as seemed best to them, but He *disciples us* for *our* good, that we may share His holiness."

5. Hebrews 12:14—"Pursue peace with all men, and the sanctification without which no one will see the Lord."

the church of God which is at Corinth, to those who have been sanctified in Christ Jesus, saints by calling . . ." All of us who are Christians are saints—but we fail at times to live up to holy standards all the time.

Reflection Questions

1. How is sanctification explained in the passages referenced in today's study?

2. Have there been times in your life that you have felt disciplined by God and did it produce in you a holier lifestyle?

3. What has the process of sanctification been like in your life lately?

22

Pleasing Sacrifices

We have an altar, from which those who serve the tabernacle have no right to eat. For the bodies of those animals whose blood is brought into the holy place by the high priest *as an offering* for sin, are burned outside the camp. Therefore Jesus also, that He might sanctify the people through His own blood, suffered outside the gate. Hence, let us go out to Him outside the camp, bearing His reproach. For here we do not have a lasting city, but we are seeking *the city* which is to come. Through Him then, let us continually offer up a sacrifice of praise to God, that is, the fruit of lips that give thanks to His name. And do not neglect doing good and sharing; for with such sacrifices God is pleased.

—HEBREWS 13:10-16

Yesterday we encountered Hebrews 9:13-14, which states: "For if the blood of goats and bulls and the ashes of a heifer sprinkling those who have been defiled, sanctify for the cleansing of the flesh, how much more will the blood of Christ, who through the eternal Spirit offered Himself without blemish to God, cleanse your conscience from dead works to serve the living God?" Through the process of cleansing, the follower of Jesus is intended to live a life of service unto God. At times this service has a sacrificial focus similar to performing ritual service at the Temple (see Romans

15:16[1]).ˣˣˣᵛ First Peter 2:5 says: "you also, as living stones, are being built up as a spiritual house for a holy priesthood, to offer up spiritual sacrifices acceptable to God through Jesus Christ"; in Hebrews 13, we are similarly called to perform sacrifices through Jesus, our high priest. Specifically, we are to provide sacrifices in the form of praise, good works, and sharing with those in need.ˣˣˣᵛⁱ

Christianity has no need for literal sacrifice, by which I mean the taking of a life in a sacrificial manner. One sacrifice, as Hebrews so eloquently argues in the first half of chapter 10, was sufficient. Thus, believers in what Jesus accomplished are called to sacrifices that do not require death beyond sacrificially dying to self or giving our lives as living sacrifices. There is similarly no longer the need to participate in other Temple procedures like offering grains or liquids to God. While it may seem innovative that believers must sacrifice or offer things to God that were not typical offerings or sacrifices according to the Israelite system, Christians are actually called to participate in a long tradition of practicing atypical sacrifices or offerings that we could call more figurative than literal.

Let me explain. First, consider Micah 6:6–8,[2] which we encountered at the start of our journey. Following the description of various possible offerings and sacrifices by which one might approach or bring delight to God, the conclusion was that God truly desired justice, faithful love, and a humble walk. Second, think about Psalm 51:16–19.[3] In the first two of these verses, the

1. Romans 15:16—"to be a minister of Christ Jesus to the Gentiles, ministering as a priest the gospel of God, that *my* offering of the Gentiles might become acceptable, sanctified by the Holy Spirit."

2. Micah 6:6–8—"With what shall I come to the Lord and bow myself before the God on high? Shall I come to Him with burnt offerings, with yearling calves? Does the Lord take delight in thousands of rams, in ten thousand rivers of oil? Shall I present my first-born *for* my rebellious acts, the fruit of my body for the sin of my soul? He has told you, O man, what is good; and what does the Lord require of you but to do justice, to love kindness, and to walk humbly with your God?"

3. Psalm 51:16–19—"For Thou dost not delight in sacrifice, otherwise I would give it; Thou art not pleased with burnt offering. The sacrifices of God are a broken spirit; a broken and a contrite heart, O God, Thou wilt not

psalmist explained that burnt-sacrifices and sacrifices were not what pleased or delighted God, but that the preferred sacrifice was a spirit that was broken. Third, read Isaiah 58 and you will see the sacrificial system turned on its head. The general idea in the Hebrew Bible as far as the subject of viewing some things as more important than rituals like sacrifices, offerings, and fasts, is that the Hebrew Bible does not obliterate the sacrificial system—in the correct circumstances, sacrifices and offerings were acceptable (see the end of the Psalm 51 quotation). Passages explain that it is more important to God to act in a correct manner before him than to go through ritual procedures as ends unto themselves, especially when lifestyles are steeped in unrepentant sin (see Isaiah 58 and Amos 5). Psalm 51 emphasizes repentance above sacrifice.

In reading several of the passages cited here, you will see that what God desired above rituals was justice. Biblical justice is related both to criminal justice (punishing wrong behaviors like murder) and social justice (looking out for the needs of others and treating others appropriately like taking care of widows). Let's think about it this way. If a widow or orphan suffers from malnutrition in my neighborhood and I did not provide any assistance when asked, I will not go to jail. I have not done anything wrong from a legal standpoint; but within the confines of social justice, I have committed an act worthy of judgement because I failed to address the needs of my suffering neighbor.

Let's go back to Hebrews 13:15–16. What types of sacrifices please God? Acts of social justice! Doing good and sharing with those in need touch the very heart of God. As priests for God, we must be engaged in sacrifices of his choosing. We must actively seek to offer up the sacrifices of helping to meet the needs of those around us.

---

despise. By Thy favor do good to Zion; build the walls of Jerusalem. Then Thou wilt delight in righteous sacrifices, in burnt offering and whole burnt offering; then young bulls will be offered on Thine altar."

Reflection Questions

1. What are we sanctified for (see Hebrews 9:13–14)?

2. How does James 1:27 relate to today's study?

3. Think about religious practices or acts of service in your own life. Have some of them lost meaning because of merely going through the motions? If so, what do you need to do about it?

23

Sanctified for Sacrifices

We have an altar, from which those who serve the tabernacle have no right to eat. For the bodies of those animals whose blood is brought into the holy place by the high priest *as an offering* for sin, are burned outside the camp. Therefore Jesus also, that He might sanctify the people through His own blood, suffered outside the gate. Hence, let us go out to Him outside the camp, bearing His reproach. For here we do not have a lasting city, but we are seeking *the city* which is to come. Through Him then, let us continually offer up a sacrifice of praise to God, that is, the fruit of lips that give thanks to His name. And do not neglect doing good and sharing; for with such sacrifices God is pleased.

—HEBREWS 13:10-16

One of the reasons for our sanctification is to serve God through sacrificial acts. Yesterday, we considered that the Israelite sacrificial system did not function properly when moral behaviors did not line up with the religious rituals. We also thought about the existence of more figurative sacrifices like a broken spirit before God. We ended with the topic of justice. Its importance, particularly social justice, in comparison to sacrificial rituals demonstrates that it touches upon matters at the very core of God's heart. The love of one's neighbor, after all, is regarded as the second of the two commandments that summarize the entire Law (Matthew 22:37–40).[1] Think about how Jesus illustrated the idea of loving one's neighbor. He did so by connecting it to social justice in the figure of the Good Samaritan (Luke 10). Jesus, the great societal reformer of his day, continued the message of the earlier prophets regarding those things that are more important than rituals.[xxxvii] In the Samaritan story, the two people who did not stop to care for the mugged and dying man were members of the priesthood (one is called a priest and the other a Levite). Why did each of them cross to the other side of the road from the injured man? The hearers of the story likely thought that not only did the characters show a lack of concern for the man, but also that the priests did not wish to become ritually impure by coming into contact with a bleeding man or even a corpse—the text mentions that the man was half-dead. He could have seemed fully dead from a distance. If such a view is correct, then Jesus intended to show in this parable that the religious clergy of his day were more concerned with ritual than caring for others. He, at the very least, explained that the religious establishment failed to love others as God commanded them to do. This stood in stark contrast to the loving actions of a Samaritan. The clergy would not have appreciated this story, for not only were the priests represented negatively in the parable, but the hero was a member of a social group deemed inferior by the Jews of Jesus' day. There was longstanding animosity towards the Samaritans that went back to as early as the Persian period (Ezra 4). Jesus sought out Samaritans, the social outcasts, for redemption (John 4). Loving those difficult to love was part of Jesus' mission and he explained that his followers must have love that extends beyond the neighbor to the point of loving those considered as enemies (Matthew 5:43–45).[2]

1. Matthew 22:37–40—"And He said to him, 'You shall love the Lord your God with all your heart, and with all your soul, and with all your mind.' This is the great and foremost commandment. The second is like it, 'You shall love your neighbor as yourself.' On these two commandments depend the whole Law and the Prophets."

2. Matthew 5:43–45—"You have heard that it was said, 'You shall love your neighbor, and hate your enemy.' But I say to you, love your enemies, and

The Good Samaritan was regarded as acting with mercy (*eleos*) in Luke 10:37,[3] which by the way is the same word used in the Greek version of Micah 6:8[4] to speak about loving mercy as one of the things that is better than sacrifice.[xxxviii] Jesus commanded the lawyer who was in dialogue with him about loving neighbors to go forth and act as the Samaritan did. The Samaritan provides a model for behaviors that fall under the categories of performing sacrifices of good works and sharing with others (Hebrews 13:16), although the sharing in Hebrews 13 seems to be specifically among Christians. I appreciate Wuest's view on the word translated in Hebrews 13:16 as "sharing." He stated that the word "in this context means 'to make one's self a sharer or partner' with someone else in his poverty or need. That is, the saints are exhorted to share what they have of earthly goods with their fellow-saints who, undergoing persecution, have been brought to a state of poverty."[xxxix]

Sharing does not come naturally. Even as children, we must be taught this foundational principle. How often do we find ourselves slipping into the old habit of "it's mine" and someone else cannot have it? Consider the following ways that I have experienced the love of Jesus working through others who shared. From my childhood days, there was the time we were loaned a one-eyed former show dog named "Joshua" to help comfort a grieving family over the loss of a beloved pet (poor Missy). As a teenager, many people generously supported my missionary excursions to far off lands, like the U.S.S.R. and the Brazilian Amazon; the malaria I received from Brazilian mosquitos was given freely, but not well appreciated. We were given a great deal of hospitality and assistance as young college newly-weds. The first house we lived in, for example, was rent-free and was about three times the size of

---

pray for those who persecute you in order that you may be sons of your Father who is in heaven; for He causes His sun to rise on *the* evil and *the* good, and sends rain on *the* righteous and *the* unrighteous."

3. Luke 10:37—"And he said, 'The one who showed mercy toward him.' And Jesus said to him, 'Go and do the same.'"

4. Micah 6:8—"He has told you, O man, what is good; and what does the Lord require of you but to do justice, to love kindness, and to walk humbly with your God?"

our current abode. In graduate school, the university graciously gave Krista a job that had the needed benefit of cafeteria food—we were the stereotypical hungry students, as seen by the fact that I lost about 30 lbs. in three months when we first moved to Israel. A close family friend also helped us significantly during our time abroad, making it possible to continue living overseas. Now as a family with young children, we have been afforded so many kind opportunities, such as using a recreational cottage on a river, staying in a condo near the beach, or being included in the holiday celebrations of other families. The evening I wrote this paragraph, friends of ours recognized a particular need in our family in the area of medical care. They were prompted by God to share this burden with us and they responded with tremendous obedience and generosity.

The examples that I have mentioned are good deeds and acts of sharing that demonstrate Christian neighborly love and while in each instance, the servants of Christ may not have recognized their actions as such, they were presenting through Christ sacrifices to God that were pleasing to him.[xl]

Reflection Questions

1. How does loving one's neighbor fit into the category of sacrifice?

2. How many acts of sacrificial good works and sharing from your own life can you list in the next five minutes? What about the ones you have done?

3. Do you find it easier to sacrifice for others or to be the recipient of sacrificial kindness? Why do you think that is the case?

24

Sanctified for Sacrifices
(Again)

We have an altar, from which those who serve the tabernacle have no right to eat. For the bodies of those animals whose blood is brought into the holy place by the high priest *as an offering* for sin, are burned outside the camp. Therefore Jesus also, that He might sanctify the people through His own blood, suffered outside the gate. Hence, let us go out to Him outside the camp, bearing His reproach. For here we do not have a lasting city, but we are seeking *the city* which is to come. Through Him then, let us continually offer up a sacrifice of praise to God, that is, the fruit of lips that give thanks to His name. And do not neglect doing good and sharing; for with such sacrifices God is pleased.

—HEBREWS 13:10-16

If you read yesterday's study, you may be wondering about the third category of sacrifice that we are made holy to perform, but which I have not emphasized. It deserves its own day. This is giving unto God sacrifices of praise. The exact phrase "sacrifice of praise" (*thusian aineseōs*) is only found in the entire Bible in this passage and in three psalms (Psalm 50:14;[1] 107:22;[2] 116:17[3]).[xli] In each of the instances from the book of Psalms, the Greek phrase appears for the Hebrew idea of thanksgiving sacrifice. The Israelite system had, for example in Leviticus 7, a ritual called a thanksgiving sacrifice in the form of slaying an animal and offering additional items. The focus was upon expressing one's appreciation to God—giving thanks. Thanksgiving sacrifices could also be coupled with offering of praise, as seen in the two poetic lines of Psalm 107:22. The first line reads: "Let them also offer sacrifices of thanksgiving"; and the second line states: "And tell of His works with joyful singing." When Hebrews 13:15 calls for praise-oriented sacrifice, it is in the form of verbal expression of thanksgiving in recognition of God.[xlii] It calls for figurative, rather than literal, sacrifice as a means of thanking God.

I must admit that Hebrews 13:15 is a helpful reminder for me to better emphasize songs of praise. Music is not my forte, but I somehow managed to court Krista with my guitar and singing. I was a pretty bad musician, though sincere in my affections. To compound my musical dysfunction, I have a difficult time memorizing songs because I am not oriented towards the auditory, unlike my oldest son. Alexander can easily memorize Scripture or the lyrics to a song through repeated listening. He can also carry a tune better than I can. I was once given a solo part in a comedy show in college, which quickly turned into a group segment to mask my less than stellar abilities.

I assume that my sincere affection was what impressed Krista despite my musical missteps. More importantly, I realize that it is neither my singing ability nor knowing the exact words of a hymn or chorus that God is after, but it is my sincere worship and adoration while presenting sacrifices of praise. A joyful song is

1. Psalm 50:14—"Offer to God a sacrifice of thanksgiving, and pay your vows to the Most High."

2. Psalm 107:22—"Let them also offer sacrifices of thanksgiving, and tell of His works with joyful singing."

3. Psalm 116:17—"To Thee I shall offer a sacrifice of thanksgiving, and call upon the name of the Lord."

what Psalm 107 prescribes and I can certainly do that. In fact, a sacrifice of praise need not be sung in every instance. It can be spoken out loud, prayed internally, written down in a journal, or read in the Bible or hymnal. If we do not faithfully praise with thanks, we rob God of a key sacrifice that he deserves. We do not perform all that we were sanctified to do. Let us, therefore, make a conscious effort today to "give thanks to the Lord" and to "call upon His name," making "known His deeds among the peoples" (1 Chronicles 16:8). Let us praise God for who he is and what he has done, especially for redeeming us through his sacrificial death.

Reflection Questions

1. What are the praiseworthy things in your life?

2. How do you prefer to present your sacrifices of praise? Perhaps it is time to try something new.

3. If you are interested, how does Colossians 3:16 relate to today's study, not just in terms of presenting a sacrifice of praise to God, but also in the sense of a sacrifice of praise benefiting fellow believers?

25

The Holy Spirit

For if the blood of goats and bulls and the ashes of a heifer sprinkling those who have been defiled, sanctify for the cleansing of the flesh, how much more will the blood of Christ, who through the eternal Spirit offered Himself without blemish to God, cleanse your conscience from dead works to serve the living God?

—HEBREWS 9:13–14

... who are chosen according to the foreknowledge of God the Father, by the sanctifying work of the Spirit, that you may obey Jesus Christ and be sprinkled with His blood: May grace and peace be yours in fullest measure.

—1 PETER 1:1B–2

We have encountered Hebrews 9:13–14 in previous studies (chapters 21 and 22). The passage, like 1 Peter 1:1–2, speaks to the sanctifying power of Jesus' blood. Both sections of Scripture talk about the holiness achieved through the sprinkling of Jesus' blood, which parallels the Israelite use of animal blood in the priestly consecration process (Exodus 29) or the application of a heifer's ashes (which included its burned blood) for purification purposes (Numbers 19). These texts mention something else of great significance.

In contemplating the sacrificial death of Jesus, I have considered on more than one occasion the role of the Holy Spirit in the process, recognizing in my heart that the Spirit was involved but I did not have any specific passage in mind. Then I came to appreciate something important about Hebrews 9:13-14. This text demonstrates the vital role played by the Holy Spirit in the sacrificial process. The Holy Spirit was the means through which Jesus sacrificed himself to God. The verbal notion of the sacrifice given here is a word (*prospherō*) that designates the giving of a sacrifice or offering in certain contexts such as this one.[xliii] Jesus is still portrayed as active in the process, but in the passage we find the third part of the Trinity explicitly involved. Thus, the Father, Son, and Holy Spirit were engaged in the sacrificial death of Jesus, who was presented as a flawless victim.

The Holy Spirit is recognized as a significant source of God's power in the world (Judges 14:6),[1] the power in Jesus' ministry (Luke 4:14),[2] and the power in the life of the early church (Acts 1:8;[3] Romans 15:13).[4] The Spirit is also the driving force behind spiritual development for Christians, leading us to deeper understandings of spiritual matters (1 Corinthians 2) and playing a key role in our sanctification (1 Corinthians 6:11; 1 Peter 1:2). Thus far in our studies, the idea of holiness has centered on the role played by Jesus' death in securing sanctification. Let's pause to consider the work of the Holy Spirit in this area, too.

1. Judges 14:6—"And the Spirit of the Lord came upon him mightily, so that he tore him as one tears a kid though he had nothing in his hand; but he did not tell his father or mother what he had done."

2. Luke 4:14—"And Jesus returned to Galilee in the power of the Spirit; and news about Him spread through all the surrounding district."

3. Acts 1:8—"'but you shall receive power when the Holy Spirit has come upon you; and you shall be My witnesses both in Jerusalem, and in all Judea and Samaria, and even to the remotest part of the earth.'"

4. Romans 15:13—"Now may the God of hope fill you with all joy and peace in believing, that you may abound in hope by the power of the Holy Spirit."

First Corinthians 6:11 is worthy of consideration; it reads: "And such were some of you; but you were washed, but you were sanctified, but you were justified in the name of the Lord Jesus Christ, and in the Spirit of our God." As presented here, the focus is not upon a process of *being* washed, sanctified, and justified, but upon those things that *have already been accomplished*. The Corinthian Christians were purified, made holy, and designated as righteous before God in Jesus' name and in the Holy Spirit. The chapter explains that the body of the Christian belongs to God and is the Holy Spirit's temple. It also references the sacrifice of Christ and gives a call to right living when it states (vs. 20): "For you have been bought with a price: therefore glorify God in your body."[xliv]

Another Pauline letter corresponds to 1 Corinthians 6 by addressing such things as correct relationships within the church, the practices that lead away from God's kingdom, and the importance of the Holy Spirit, that is, the book of Galatians. It would be worthwhile to provide a quotation of Galatians 5:16–26, but that would be too lengthy. It is a section that contrasts fleshly works to the Holy Spirit's fruit, declares that our flesh has been crucified, and states (5:16): "But I say, walk by the Spirit, and you will not carry out the desire of the flesh." Thus, it is by walking according to the ways of the Holy Spirit that we are able to give glory to God in our bodies and to bear that life-oriented fruit with such outstanding aspects as love and joy and peace and much more. Given the primacy of love, as in the greatest commandments or its identification as more significant than other good things (Col 3:14),[5] it is no wonder that love starts the list of attributes of the Spirit's fruit. Love is of the greatest importance.

Reflection Questions

1. What is the role of the Holy Spirit in the life of the Christian?

5. Colossians 3:14—"And beyond all these things *put on* love, which is the perfect bond of unity."

2. How is the Spirit's power portrayed in the passages cited or quoted in today's study?

3. Do a self-inventory using Galatians 5:16–26. As a person consecrated to God who is in the process of developing stronger God-oriented character by walking with the Holy Spirit, what fleshly deeds are you indulging and what aspects of the Spirit's fruit are you seeing in your daily life? Try memorizing the contrasting lists in verses 19 to 23 to help you stay focused or pick something from the lists to work on through the Holy Spirit's power.

26

Walking in the Light

And this is the message we have heard from Him and announce to you, that God is light, and in Him there is no darkness at all. If we say that we have fellowship with Him and *yet* walk in the darkness, we lie and do not practice the truth; but if we walk in the light as He Himself is in the light, we have fellowship with one another, and the blood of Jesus His Son cleanses us from all sin. If we say that we have no sin, we are deceiving ourselves, and the truth is not in us. If we confess our sins, He is faithful and righteous to forgive us our sins and to cleanse us from all unrighteousness. If we say that we have not sinned, we make Him a liar, and His word is not in us.

—1 JOHN 1:5–10

Previously we encountered the continuation of this discussion when we examined Jesus' role as our advocate when we sin (1 John 2). It is fitting to consider 1 John 1 in today's study because of its representation of walking in the light. To remain in the light requires walking in close fellowship with the Holy Spirit. It results in abiding in the same space inhabited by God, who is light according to 1 John 1. The martyr Stephen (Acts 6) lived a Spirit-filled life. To have such a life means that we must walk in submission to the Holy Spirit to such an extent that we are living in a manner that yields to God and not fleshly desire. It is surrender to God, rather than self-indulgence. It is empowerment, rather than defeat.

There is more. An important role of the Holy Spirit is to convict of sin (John 16:8).[1] Walking in the Spirit, which is being in the light, exposes our sins. To deny the existence of sinful behavior in our lives or to practice sin intentionally is to walk in the darkness (see also 1 John 2:9–10).[2] As we are sensitive to the Spirit's conviction, then we are led to confess our sins to God, resulting in forgiveness and cleansing by Jesus' blood. There is great reason to hope because of this passage, for it clearly acknowledges that moral missteps are made, but they are addressed through confession and the application of Jesus' blood (see Ephesians 1:7–8A;[3] Revelation 1:5[4]).[xlv] The text speaks of the Father's faithfulness and justness to forgive and to cleanse when we confess to him. In a single moment the burden of sin and guilt is eradicated. The problem we face at times is that we lack faith that the forgiveness and cleansing have been applied. We get stuck in the muck of self-condemnation. A bog that I know all too well. There are other times when we quickly recognize or accept that we have been pardoned. We move forward in the peace that comes from the removal of the burden of sin and guilt.

Being under the light of conviction can be a very uncomfortable place to be until the situation is resolved. There are times that we also need to confess to people. I had a few circumstances transpire this past summer in which past errors I committed were brought to mind and required confession to the individuals I

1. John 16:8—"And He, when He comes, will convict the world concerning sin, and righteousness, and judgment."

2. 1 John 2:9–10—"The one who says he is in the light and *yet* hates his brother is in the darkness until now. The one who loves his brother abides in the light and there is no cause for stumbling in him."

3. Ephesians 1:7–8a—"In Him we have redemption through His blood, the forgiveness of our trespasses, according to the riches of His grace, which he lavished upon us."

4. Revelation 1:5—"and from Jesus Christ, the faithful witness, the first-born of the dead, and the ruler of the kings of the earth. To Him who loves us, and released us from our sins by His blood."

wronged. While one of the situations related to sinful behavior, the other did not. Both, however, were errors in judgment that did not cause me any conviction when the errors were being committed. I did not realize that I had done anything wrong. It is a strange and troubling sensation when the light of truth finally goes on and you discover that something is not right. Ignorance is bliss, it is said, and it truly is. There is also the opposite problem of over-analyzing things and perceiving errors when there are none. Unfortunately, my errors did occur and I felt ashamed. I confessed to the relevant people and received their forgiveness.

Obtaining forgiveness is one of the greatest human experiences. In one of the circumstances that I was just taking about, the emotional response to the release from guilt was powerful and it struck me as being much like the forgiveness one receives from God. The recognition of past and present sin comes as we walk with the Holy Spirit in God's light. Confession of these wrongs when walking in communion with God leads to forgiveness. It is guaranteed.

Sensitivity to conviction in a given moment can save us from making mistakes. Being in the light is not just about conviction. It is about so much more. It is about living in communion with God and following the correct path set out before us. Through the leading of the Spirit, we can bask in the light instead of groping around in the darkness.

Reflection Questions

1. Do you find it easier to confess to God or to other people? How might the Holy Spirit be leading you to confess today?

2. What is the promised result of your confessions, as given in today's passage?

3. In what other ways is God leading today?

27

Called to Holiness and Redeemed with Precious Blood

As to this salvation, the prophets who prophesied of the grace that *would come* to you made careful search and inquiry, seeking to know what person or time the Spirit of Christ within them was indicating as He predicted the sufferings of Christ and the glories to follow. It was revealed to them that they were not serving themselves, but you, in these things which now have been announced to you through those who preached the gospel to you by the Holy Spirit sent from heaven—things into which angels long to look. Therefore, gird your minds for action, keep sober *in spirit,* fix your hope completely on the grace to be brought to you at the revelation of Jesus Christ. As obedient children, do not be conformed to the former lusts *which were yours* in your ignorance, but like the Holy One who called you, be holy yourselves also in all *your* behavior; because it is written, "You shall be holy, for I am holy." And if you address as Father the One who impartially judges according to each man's work, conduct yourselves in fear during the time of your stay *upon earth*; knowing that you were not redeemed with perishable things like silver or gold from your futile way of life inherited from your forefathers, but with precious blood, as of a lamb unblemished and spotless, *the blood* of Christ.

—1 PETER 1:10-19

These verses make a lengthy quotation, but they correspond to several ideas addressed in our previous studies, so let's refresh our memories:

First, the Holy Spirit is mentioned as serving an instrumental role in guiding such figures as prophets and those who proclaimed the gospel message to the recipients of the letter. Notice the prophets are not represented here as simply passive recipients of information, but that they were earnest in seeking out truth. There are times when we must diligently seek, which may require careful inquiry and study.

Second, the above text states that believers must get their minds dressed and ready for action, practicing sobriety, with hope set on God's favor or grace. We have seen that grace is the basis of salvation. We hope not in justification through works, but in God's favorable generosity, including the Son's sacrificial death.

Third, the recipients of the letter were told not to conform to old sinful practices that came from ignorance, but to live out holy lives in order to be like God. Sanctification is a process and requires a conscious effort to move away from the things of the old self, slaying the ways of the flesh.

Fourth, 1 Peter tells the Christ-follower to live in healthy fear of a divine court date. Such a fear should motivate one to choose right actions, but such a fear should be tempered by the lack of condemnation that, as we saw, is promised to those in Christ. There is an advocate to represent the Christian before the Father.

Fifth, 1 Peter refers to the idea of redemption. It does so to contrast the Israelite sacrificial system to the sacrifice of Jesus. The idea also occurs in the book of Exodus. In Exodus 13:11–15,[1] a

1. Exodus 13:11–15—"Now it shall come about when the Lord brings you to the land of the Canaanite, as He swore to you and to your fathers, and gives it to you, that you shall devote to the Lord the first offspring of every womb, and the first offspring of every beast that you own; the males belong to the Lord. But every first offspring of a donkey you shall redeem with a lamb, but if you do not redeem *it*, then you shall break its neck; and every first-born of man among your sons you shall redeem. And it shall be when your son asks you in time to come, saying, 'What is this?' then you shall say to him, 'With a powerful hand the Lord brought us out of Egypt, from the house of slavery. And it came about, when Pharaoh was stubborn about letting us go, that the

father is told about the manner in which he should tell a firstborn son the reason behind the need to ransom him. The father must describe to his son that at the time the Egyptian Pharaoh denied Israelite freedom, God killed the firstborn humans and animals in Egypt. This is why the father must sacrifice every firstborn of his herd or flock (it belongs to God), but redeem the firstborn son.[xlvi] When Passover began, the blood of lambs or goats,[xlvii] applied to doorframes, ransomed the firstborn sons of Israel. The Israelites were commanded to continue ransoming their firstborn sons to commemorate the Exodus events.[xlviii] Annual Passover practices also remember the Exodus, which has been viewed as the greatest act of redemption for early Israel. As we will discuss later in our reflections, Passover is considered by the Church as the time of the greatest act of redemption in global history: the sacrifice of a human Passover lamb. It was the blood of Jesus that secured the redemption (1 Peter 1:19). For early Jewish Christians, Jesus' redemptive work as a symbolic Passover lamb may have had two key connotations since Jesus could be seen as the substitutional lamb that replaced the firstborn humans (as in the Exodus ritual), and also as the redeeming agent who purchased people destined for death (as in the post-Exodus tradition of ransoming firstborn sons).

I hope and pray that you are gaining a better appreciation for the foundational truths we have been reflecting upon during our time together. Do you see how several of the matters addressed so far are connected, revolving around the sacrificial death of Jesus Christ?

Reflection Questions

1. What are some similarities and differences between the way 1 Peter 1 represents the sacrificial death of Jesus in comparison to other passages we have encountered?

Lord killed every first-born in the land of Egypt, both the first-born of man and the first-born of beast. Therefore, I sacrifice to the Lord the males, the first offspring of every womb, but every first-born of my sons I redeem.'"

2. What type of responses are required of us based upon the passage under consideration for today?

3. Why must we strive to be holy? Through God's help, have you made some progress in certain behaviors lately?

28

Unable to Give, Denying Ourselves

And He *continued* by questioning them, 'But who do you say that I am?' Peter answered and said to Him, 'Thou art the Christ.' And He warned them to tell no one about Him. And He began to teach them that the Son of Man must suffer many things and be rejected by the elders and the chief priests and the scribes, and be killed, and after three days rise again. And He was stating the matter plainly. And Peter took Him aside and began to rebuke Him. But turning around and seeing His disciples, He rebuked Peter, and said, "Get behind Me, Satan; for you are not setting your mind on God's interests, but man's." And He summoned the multitude with His disciples, and said to them, "If anyone wishes to come after Me, let him deny himself, and take up his cross, and follow Me. For whoever wishes to save his life shall lose it; but whoever loses his life for My sake and the gospel's shall save it. For what does it profit a man to gain the whole world, and forfeit his soul? For what shall a man give in exchange for his soul? For whoever is ashamed of Me and My words in this adulterous and sinful generation, the Son of Man will also be ashamed of him when He comes in the glory of His Father with the holy angels."

—MARK 8:29–38

These verses explain one of the most pivotal moments in the Gospel narratives. Jesus was in the extreme northern part of Israel with his disciples. Mount Hermon was looming large as Peter made a monumental declaration that Jesus was the long-awaited Messiah or Christ. Peter's sense of triumph in correctly identifying Jesus' role must have faded quickly when Jesus denounced Peter in front of the other disciples. Jesus did this because Peter had criticized him upon hearing that it was necessary for Jesus to suffer and die. It is understandable that Peter was disturbed by Jesus' declaration that he would be executed. He, and his fellow Jews, were primarily expecting a Messiah to conquer and to rule, not one who would be dominated and killed by the rulers of the day. In Jesus' rebuke to Peter, the reason given for the reprimand is important when considering where the passage leads. Jesus explained that Peter was focused on human interests, not God's. This is precisely what is at stake when we are faced with self-denial. Jesus told his closest disciples and everyone else following him that the cost of discipleship was extreme, but paradoxical. It is like Jesus' teaching that if a person wishes to be a leader, they must be a servant. In this episode, the followers were told that *death* to self results in *true life*.

One of Jesus' statements reminds me of Micah's questioning concerning what could be given as a means of addressing his sin (6:6–8).[1] Jesus asked what a person could provide in order to barter for the soul (Mark 8:37),[2] with the potential implication of what sacrifice could be given. The answer is nothing, except turning a person's life over to God. A life could be found (Matthew 16:25)[3]

---

1. Micah 6:6–8—"With what shall I come to the Lord and bow myself before the God on high? Shall I come to Him with burnt offerings, with yearling calves? Does the Lord take delight in thousands of rams, in ten thousand rivers of oil? Shall I present my first-born *for* my rebellious acts, the fruit of my body for the sin of my soul? He has told you, O man, what is good; and what does the Lord require of you but to do justice, to love kindness, and to walk humbly with your God?"

2. Mark 8:37—"For what shall a man give in exchange for his soul?"

3. Matthew 16:25—"For whoever wishes to save his life shall lose it; but whoever loses his life for My sake shall find it."

or saved (Mark 8:35;[4] Luke 9:23–24)[5] by self-denial for the sake of the kingdom of God. Jesus likened this self-denial to picking up the implement of destruction: a cross. The emphasis is placed on a continual or daily (Luke 9:23) process of self-elimination. While physical death is not the primarily focus of Jesus' teaching about self-denial, martyrdom was a possibility that turned into reality for the early church. In other places of the New Testament, the type of self-denial mentioned by Jesus is expressed explicitly in sacrificial terms, but that is not the issue here.

Reflecting upon today's topic as it relates to my own life, I would say that there have been moments when I have been better at self-denial, but there have been times when I have served others while grumbling internally. There have also been situations in which I have been thinking about how my service might benefit me and I have arrogantly relished in how good it is of me to do something for another person. So even when I externally deny myself, I may still be selfishly seeking my own interests. This is where the rebuke of Peter fits into the equation. Peter's focus turned to human interests, not kingdom affairs. Perhaps he lay awake at night, dreaming of the glories he might experience under the Messiah's earthly reign; or maybe he had more noble concerns related to the death of his rabbi. In any case, he did not understand the importance and necessity of Jesus' sacrificial death.

Peter was concerned with earthly consequences perceived through self-interest. We can relate. We all struggle with selfish desires connected to gaining the things of this world, and sometimes we think our ambitions are noble, even pure. At times, they are. At other times, our supposedly lofty goals are simply manifestations of self-centeredness. Only through God's help can we truly deny ourselves and be devoted disciples.

4. Mark 8:35—"For whoever wishes to save his life shall lose it, but whoever loses his life for My sake and the gospel's shall save it."

5. Luke 9:23–24—"And He was saying to *them* all, 'If anyone wishes to come after Me, let him deny himself, and take up his cross daily, and follow Me. For whoever wishes to save his life shall lose it, but whoever loses his life for My sake, he is the one who will save it.'"

Reflection Questions

1. How does today's passage express the danger of living a life focused on worldly pursuits?

2. How difficult do you find it to practice self-denial and how is God directing you today along such a path?

3. Meditate upon Matthew 6:25–34. How can you better incorporate Matthew 6:33 into your life today?

29

Crucified with Christ

What shall we say then? Are we to continue in sin that grace might increase? May it never be! How shall we who died to sin still live in it? Or do you not know that all of us who have been baptized into Christ Jesus have been baptized into His death? Therefore we have been buried with Him through baptism into death, in order that as Christ was raised from the dead through the glory of the Father, so we too might walk in newness of life. For if we have become united with *Him* in the likeness of His death, certainly we shall be also *in the likeness* of His resurrection, knowing this, that our old self was crucified with *Him,* that our body of sin might be done away with, that we should no longer be slaves to sin; for he who has died is freed from sin.

—ROMANS 6:1-7

This passage comes right after the explanation of such concepts as justification, the conquest of transgression through Jesus, and the comparison between the death that results from sin and the life that comes through grace (Romans 5). Now, Romans 6, which relates to Galatians 2 as well, calls for a response to these truths with a focus upon the ending of sinful behaviors in light of the identification of the Christian with the death, burial, and resurrection of Christ.

This chapter has special significance for me. Krista and I have been blessed with the opportunity to participate in some very meaningful Easter sunrise services, such as one that took place many years ago on the Mount of Olives in Jerusalem. Instead of focusing on those, today I reflect upon a very recent service, not because of the location but because of a momentous event that transpired. We took our boys to celebrate a sunrise service at a local beach. People were packed into the worship space on the pier and the service was amplified over a speaker system. It was not necessarily the contemplative time that was expected by all of the members of my family, so we walked down to the beach to spend some time freer from the confines of the service space. As we moved, Romans 6 was being read and the text struck me like it never had before. Shortly thereafter, my youngest son, Gabriel, decided to get baptized. He was spiritually ready, the cold ocean water was available, and some kind strangers joined our little family service, documenting the occasion with pictures. Krista and I were ready, too. We were relatively experienced baptizers, having performed the lakeside baptism of our oldest son, Alexander.

As the sun was rising and with a sky brightened with shades of yellow, green, and blue, Gabriel joined in a 2000 plus year old ritual, identifying him with the death, burial, and resurrection of Jesus. Thus, with Romans 6 (as quoted above), I can declare that Gabriel's "old self was crucified with [Jesus], that [his] body of sin might be done away with, that [he] should no longer be [a slave] to sin; for he who has died is freed from sin." I can say this of Alexander, Krista, and me. If you are a Christian reading this, insert your name in the text. Make it personal. One of the key ramifications for me and for you is that while we must still live in our bodies for the time being, our flesh has been slain in a spiritual sense. It has been killed to the extent that the bondage of sin no longer enslaves us as it did before. There is more to it, however, as Romans 6:12–14[1] explains. We must not give sin the position of

1. Romans 6:12–14—"Therefore do not let sin reign in your mortal body

ruler that it seeks. It is defeated, but we can still allow it to serve as a usurper sitting upon the throne of our lives. We must present our bodies to God in his service as our legitimate king, and not to sin. This is self-denial and it is the process of sanctification at work, as the end of Romans 6:19 states: "so now present your members *as* slaves to righteousness, resulting in sanctification" (see 6:22).[2] It takes divine empowerment through the Holy Spirit and human determination. We cannot do it on our own.

Reflection Questions

1. What does baptism mean to you? Is it merely a public declaration of faith or is there more involved?

2. What does it mean to be crucified with Jesus and what is the result of participating in his death?

3. Name three places where you are allowing sin to creep in and what should you do about it?

---

that you should obey its lusts, and do not go on presenting the members of your body to sin *as* instruments of unrighteousness; but present yourselves to God as those alive from the dead, and your members *as* instruments of righteousness to God. For sin shall not be master over you, for you are not under law, but under grace."

2. Romans 6:22—"But now having been freed from sin and enslaved to God, you derive your benefit, resulting in sanctification, and the outcome, eternal life."

30

Crucified with Christ (Again)

I have been crucified with Christ; and it is no longer I who live, but
Christ lives in me; and the *life* which I now live in the flesh I live by
faith in the Son of God, who loved me, and delivered Himself up
for me. I do not nullify the grace of God; for if righteousness *comes*
through the Law, then Christ died needlessly.

—GALATIANS 2:20-21

I realize that we have covered this passage previously, but we did
not adequately discuss the matter of being crucified with Jesus.
I am fond of the passage and I am also intrigued by its teachings,
which correspond closely to those in Romans 6 about the crucifixion of the flesh and the reception of life in Christ. I memorized
Galatians 2:20 decades ago, but I have only recently come to a better appreciation of it. I am still in the process of understanding the
passage and seeking to live out its message.

Paul, as explained in Galatians 2 and elsewhere, believed that
he was no longer his own man and that he had no right to himself, considering that the Christ-follower was "freed from sin and
enslaved to God" through the death, burial, and resurrection (Romans 6:22). In addition, Paul wrote: "For to me, to live is Christ,
and to die is gain" (Philippians 1:21). It would seem that he pos-
sessed a singular focus that went beyond the recognition that the

self was crucified with Christ. He was determined to live out that reality practically. Paul's focus was explained in Philippians as a determination to leave the past behind while focusing on what was in front of him to the extent that he pressed forward to grab ahold of "the prize of the upward call of God in Christ Jesus" (3:14). It is in this same section that we read of Paul's passion to know Jesus and to conform to the crucifixion (3:7–10):

> But whatever things were gain to me, those things I have counted as loss for the sake of Christ. More than that, I count all things to be loss in view of the surpassing value of knowing Christ Jesus my Lord, for whom I have suffered the loss of all things, and count them but rubbish in order that I may gain Christ, and may be found in Him, not having a righteousness of my own derived from *the* Law, but that which is through faith in Christ, the righteousness which *comes* from God on the basis of faith, that I may know Him, and the power of His resurrection and the fellowship of His sufferings, being conformed to His death.

These are powerful words spoken by a man who embodied Jesus' call to self-denial and cross bearing. The reality that we have been crucified with Jesus requires that we abide by the recognition that we no longer have ownership over the life we often consider our own. At the end of Galatians, Paul noted that he desired only to boast in the cross "through which the world has been crucified to me, and I to the world" (6:14). Due to persecution, he came to reflect the sufferings of Jesus literally. His flesh carried the markings of Jesus (6:17).[1] Sadly many Christians today bear similar scars of persecution for the sake of Christ.

---

1. Galatians 6:17—"From now on let no one cause trouble for me, for I bear on my body the brand-marks of Jesus."

Reflection Questions

1. How should Galatians 2:20 change our perspective on life? If you are like me, I could use an hourly reminder of the content of this verse.

2. In what ways are you still struggling to surrender control to God even though we have been crucified with Jesus?

3. Paul had a clear sense of his calling and he was determined to follow it no matter the cost. How would you define your calling in God? How can you press forward more fully in fulfilling that calling?

3 1

Presenting Our Bodies

I urge you therefore, brethren, by the mercies of God, to present
your bodies a living and holy sacrifice, acceptable to God, *which is*
your spiritual service of worship. And do not be conformed to this
world, but be transformed by the renewing of your mind, that you
may prove what the will of God is, that which is good and acceptable
and perfect.

—ROMANS 12:1–2

We have already studied in Romans 6 the practical advice for
how to live in the reality that the flesh has been crucified
and a new life has been granted. This is by ceasing to present our
body parts to perform sinful things. Followers of Jesus should instead present themselves to God and their body parts to righteous
acts (6:12–14).[1] The second part of Romans 6:19 adds the following statements: "For just as you presented your members *as* slaves
to impurity and to lawlessness, resulting in *further* lawlessness, so
now present your members *as* slaves to righteousness, resulting in

1. Romans 6:12–14—"Therefore do not let sin reign in your mortal body
that you should obey its lusts, and do not go on presenting the members of
your body to sin *as* instruments of unrighteousness; but present yourselves
to God as those alive from the dead, and your members *as* instruments of
righteousness to God. For sin shall not be master over you, for you are not
under law, but under grace."

sanctification." In Romans 6, the concept of presenting (*paristēmi*) is conceptualized in terms of the relationship between slave and master. It does not have sacrificial implications. For Romans 12:1–2, however, the notion of presenting is represented in a sacrificial context with the sense of an act of dedication.[xlix] Thus, a person must dedicate the body as a living sacrifice, which is holy and well-pleasing to God. Such an act is regarded as a type of sacrificial service (*latreia*),[l] just like the type of service performed at the Israelite Tabernacle or Temple (Hebrews 9:6).[2] The service that the passage dictates for the reader is a figurative sacrifice of self, rather than the literal sacrifices performed at the Temple.[li]

Being a living sacrifice is not only paradoxical, for the point of sacrifice is death, but it is also extremely difficult. It requires surrender, vigilance, determination, commitment, concentration, and much more. A significant amount of divine assistance is needed because on the one hand, the default setting in our minds is selfishness, and on the other, our natural capacity to dedicate every single moment to sacrificial surrender is impossible. When we fail to concentrate on sacrificially living for God, we slip into our default mode of self-fulfillment. It is fitting, therefore, that Romans 12 moves from encouraging living sacrificially to a focus on having a transformation linked to the mind's renewal. It is a renewal in contrast to being conformed to the ways of this age. It is this renewal that allows us to live sacrificially. We cannot do it on our own.

Consider how Colossians 3 corresponds to Romans 12:2, when it explains how the Christian must have a mind focused on heavenly matters, regard the earthly body as dead to sin, and put away sinful behaviors. This is because the old self has been set aside and the new self has been put on, which is in the process of "being renewed to a true knowledge according to the image of the One who created him" (3:10). Humanity was created in the image

---

2. Hebrews 9:6—"Now when these things have been thus prepared, the priests are continually entering the outer tabernacle, performing the divine worship."

of God (Genesis 1:27),[3] but sin has affected us. We do not, for example, perceive things and react to them as we were meant to. We need our minds renewed so that we better mirror God's mind.

According to 2 Corinthians 4:16,[4] the inner renewal is occurring daily; Titus 3:5[lii] explains that the process is linked to the work of the Holy Spirit; 2 Corinthians 3:18[5] similarly speaks to the Spirit's role in transforming Christians into the glorious image of God; and Romans 8:29 deals with the idea of conformity (rather than renewal) to the image of Christ. In light of the preceding verse (Romans 8:28),[6] one could go so far as to consider that an aspect of how everything in the life of the believer works in a positive manner, is that the circumstances of life assist us in the transformation/conformation/renewal process so that we can reflect the image of Jesus more closely. This is the process of sanctification at work.

Reflection Questions

1. Read through Colossians 3 and Romans 12. Write down a list of similarities and differences in terms of the behaviors that each passage endorses and condemns.

2. What negative or positive behaviors that are addressed in Romans 12 or Colossians 3 require some additional attention in your life?

3. Genesis 1:27—"And God created man in His own image, in the image of God He created him; male and female He created them."

4. 2 Corinthians 4:16—"Therefore we do not lose heart, but though our outer man is decaying, yet our inner man is being renewed day by day."

5. 2 Corinthians 3:18—"But we all, with unveiled face beholding as in a mirror the glory of the Lord, are being transformed into the same image from glory to glory, just as from the Lord, the Spirit."

6. Romans 8:28-29—"And we know that God causes all things to work together for good to those who love God, to those who are called according to *His* purpose. For whom He foreknew, He also predestined *to become* conformed to the image of His Son, that He might be the firstborn among many brethren."

3. What practical step can you take today to be a living sacrifice more consistently? Set an hourly reminder to pray through Romans 12:1–2? Make a point to speak with someone else about the verses? Write out the passage on your forearm? Be creative.

32

The Mind of Christ

If therefore there is any encouragement in Christ, if there is any consolation of love, if there is any fellowship of the Spirit, if any affection and compassion, make my joy complete by being of the same mind, maintaining the same love, united in spirit, intent on one purpose. Do nothing from selfishness or empty conceit, but with humility of mind let each of you regard one another as more important than himself; do not *merely* look out for your own personal interests, but also for the interests of others. Have this attitude in yourselves which was also in Christ Jesus, who, although He existed in the form of God, did not regard equality with God a thing to be grasped, but emptied Himself, taking the form of a bond-servant, *and* being made in the likeness of men. And being found in appearance as a man, He humbled Himself by becoming obedient to the point of death, even death on a cross.

—PHILIPPIANS 2:1–8

As we become less conformed to worldly affairs and more transformed through our minds' renewal, we will better reflect the mindset of Christ and thereby live sacrificially like him. In the passage quoted above, there is an emphasis upon appropriate ways to think. The first is in the area of like-mindedness within the church. The church is regarded as a unified body; having sameness in mind is a fitting concept. The unified nature of the church is one of the focal points in Colossians 3 and Romans 12 as well. The latter speaks to the diversity of gifting within the church, but that there exists an overall unity. The former goes so far as to indicate that social and ethnic distinctions are erased in Jesus, the central uniting element of the church.

The second aspect of correct thinking relates to interpersonal relations, emphasizing the avoidance of self-centeredness and conceit. Instead of preference for self, we should have a humble attitude that diminishes self-importance in favor of others. We should similarly seek to address those things that are important to others. The third matter corresponds to being like-minded with Jesus, who modeled humble self-denial and servitude in the incarnation and crucifixion. The way that Jesus lived out the sacrificial mindset in the context of first century Israel/Palestine became the model for Christian sacrificial living. Such a sacrificial mindset is demonstrated by Paul in this chapter of Philippians.

As chapter 2 continues beyond the verses quoted above, additional instructions are provided to the church at Philippi, promoting in Paul the desire that the church should remain faithful lest it be shown that his labor was in vain. Still, he believed that there was merit in his efforts, stating: "But even if I am being poured out as a drink offering upon the sacrifice and service of your faith, I rejoice and share my joy with you all" (Philippians 2:17).[liii] The practice of adding a liquid offering or libation to an animal sacrifice (see Numbers 28:15)[1] is the imagery evoked here—picture an act of pouring out a precious liquid like wine to God. That is what Paul had in mind.

Paul considered the pouring out of his life as an offering to be a matter of jubilation. Such a perspective corresponds to the mindset of Christ. Paul was spending himself for the benefit of others and he was pleased to do so. Sacrificial self-denial need not be a

---

1. Numbers 28:15—"And one male goat for a sin offering to the Lord; it shall be offered with its libation in addition to the continual burnt offering."

dreary affair, but it requires a renewed point of view to consider it in a positive light.

Reflection Questions

1. Do you find yourself responding more often in either a positive or negative way to doing things for others? What does that say about your mindset?

2. What was the basis for Paul's joy in being a human libation?

3. Read Colossians 3:17 and 23. What practical advice is given in those verses for laboring under the right mindset?

33

Eating the Sacrificially Given Bread of Life

"I am the bread of life. Your fathers ate the manna in the wilderness, and they died. This is the bread which comes down out of heaven, so that one may eat of it and not die. I am the living bread that came down out of heaven; if anyone eats of this bread, he shall live forever; and the bread also which I shall give for the life of the world is My flesh." The Jews therefore *began* to argue with one another, saying, "How can this man give us *His* flesh to eat?" Jesus therefore said to them, "Truly, truly, I say to you, unless you eat the flesh of the Son of Man and drink His blood, you have no life in yourselves. He who eats My flesh and drinks My blood has eternal life, and I will raise him up on the last day. For my flesh is true food, and My blood is true drink. He who eats my flesh and drinks My blood abides in Me, and I in him."

—JOHN 6:48–56

Jesus' statements about being life-giving bread are contextualized in the events occurring soon after feeding 5000 plus people at Passover time in Galilee. People flocked to Jesus' presence and he said to them that it was not due to observing miracles that they followed him, but because he fed them. He then told them not to seek out perishable food, but rather to pursue the type of food that lasts unto everlasting life, that is, the food that comes from him (John 6:26–27).[1] This is an important concept that reminds me of Jesus' teachings in Matthew 6:33[2] regarding the need to focus on God's kingdom instead of our material needs. I must admit that at the time of writing today's study, I felt that I failed to live out John 6:27 even though the passage was right in front of me and Matthew 6 was also on my mind. I will avoid the details, but the essence of what occurred is that I chose to make an appearance at a work-related event that I could have skipped. I did this instead of working on today's passage because I wanted to make a positive impression that could lead to a financial benefit in the long run. We certainly should seek out excellence in the workplace, but in this particular instance, I chose to seek earthly rewards instead of heavenly affairs even though I was under conviction to continue working on John 6. I sensed that just as Jesus tested Philip when he asked about how the multitude would be fed (John 6:5–7),[3] I, too, was being tested. Philip did not pass the test either.

Jesus presented his controversial teachings about his origins, his equivalency to life-giving bread, and the importance of his blood to those gathered at the Capernaum synagogue. Some disciples, apparently not the twelve main disciples, responded that what he taught was too difficult to accept. The text indicates that this was a breaking point for some of the disciples, who abandoned their commitment to follow Jesus as their rabbi; the twelve remained. In truth, what Jesus said would be hard for most anyone, let alone a synagogue filled with first century Jews, who at Passover

1. John 6:26–27—"Jesus answered them and said, 'Truly, truly, I say to you, you seek Me, not because you saw signs, but because you ate of the loaves, and were filled. Do not work for the food which perishes, but for the food which endures to eternal life, which the Son of Man shall give to you, for on Him the Father, *even* God, has set His seal.'"

2. Matthew 6:33—"But seek first His kingdom and His righteousness; and all these things shall be added to you."

3. John 6:5–7—"Jesus therefore lifting up His eyes, and seeing that a great multitude was coming to Him, said to Philip, 'Where are we to buy bread, that these may eat?' And this He was saying to test him; for He Himself knew what He was intending to do. Philip answered Him, 'Two hundred denarii worth of bread is not sufficient for them, for everyone to receive a little.'"

time were mindful of the eating of sacrificial meat and the use of blood on doorframes. What Jesus articulated sounded like cannibalism, as well as something that went against the very core of keeping kosher, which is the avoidance of consuming blood.[liv] Jesus, however, was speaking metaphorically to note that coming to him and believing in him, as well as his teachings, were akin to eating his body and drinking his blood. Such a meaning behind Jesus' difficult comments can be deduced from the wider context of John 6 (see, for example, 6:63[4] also 68[5]).[lv] One of the key concepts that required belief was in his sacrificial death, which Jesus explained in John 6:51 in terms of sacrificially giving (*didōmi*) his flesh "for the life of the world." Hence, Jesus was a substitution: a life given in exchange for another. Such exchange is at the heart of Passover. That Jesus spoke these words at Passover foreshadows his later creation of the Lord's Supper or Communion or Eucharist.

Reflection Questions

1. Read through John 6. What are you seeking from Jesus?

2. With whom in the chapter do you most identify? Have there been times in your life during which you were more like the multitude, the close companions of Jesus, or the other disciples who walked away?

3. Can you recall a time that you have you been spiritually tested? How can we be better prepared to respond to situations that leave us at a crossroads between choosing earthly food or heavenly manna?

4. John 6:63—"It is the Spirit who gives life; the flesh profits nothing; the words that I have spoken to you are spirit and are life."

5. John 6:68—"Simon Peter answered Him, 'Lord, to whom shall we go? You have words of eternal life.'"

34

Flesh and Blood

And when He had taken *some* bread *and* given thanks, He broke *it*,
and gave *it* to them, saying, "This is My body which is given for you;
do this in remembrance of Me." And in the same way *He took* the
cup after they had eaten, saying, "This cup which is poured out for
you is the new covenant in my blood."

—LUKE 22:19-20

And while they were eating, He took *some* bread, and after a blessing He broke *it;* and gave *it* to them, and said, "Take *it;* this is My
body." And when He had taken a cup, *and* given thanks, He gave *it* to
them; and they all drank from it. And He said to them, "This is My
blood of the covenant, which is poured out for many."

—MARK 14:22-24

I find John's account of the teachings of Christ about his flesh and
blood intriguing from the standpoint of timing. The Passover
meal of the Last Supper is where the other Gospel narratives speak
about such matters, but Jesus' final meal with his disciples in John's
Gospel does not (John 13-17). Thus, Jesus taught in Capernaum
at an earlier Passover time about his body and blood as something

to consume, and also in Jerusalem at the Passover during which he was crucified. It was at this final Passover that Jesus initiated the new ritual that would transform the Passover meal into a key reminder of his sacrificial death. He took the bread and wine, designating them as his body and blood to be ingested. While belief was involved, a physical rite was provided that was not referenced in the Capernaum teaching.

The three other Gospels (Matthew, Mark, and Luke) present Jesus' transformation of the Passover meal with some variation. Matthew, for instance, records that Jesus' blood was being used to obtain forgiveness from sin (see tomorrow's study). Luke's account indicates that Jesus specified that his body was being given sacrificially (*didōmi*), an idea lacking in the other two Gospels. Luke, too, records that Jesus commanded that eating the bread should be done to remember him. First Corinthians also references remembrance but in terms of eating the bread and drinking the wine (11:23–26).[1] Such commemoration provided new meaning to the Passover, which was already a memorial festival to begin with. It was a time to remember the dramatic redemption of the Israelites from the clutches of Egypt after a final act of plague: the death of the firstborn. The life of the Passover lamb substituted for the life of the firstborn; and the animal's blood, which covered the doorframe, served as a covering for the firstborn of the house by designating the space as off limits for death. The redemption of the Israelites from Egypt is one of the most remembered moments of deliverance throughout the Hebrew Bible. Time and time again, it is brought forth (e.g., Psalm 136). It was the start of a new era with a new covenant that would serve as the basis of Israelite religion from antiquity unto contemporary Judaism. So, too, has Jesus' covenant been for the early church until this day. Each time the Lord's

---

1. 1 Corinthians 11:23–26—"For I received from the Lord that which I also delivered to you, that the Lord Jesus in the night in which He was betrayed took bread; and when He had given thanks, He broke it, and said, 'This is My body, which is for you; do this in remembrance of Me.' In the same way He *took* the cup also, after supper, saying, 'This cup is the new covenant in My blood; do this, as often as you drink *it*, in remembrance of Me.' For as often as you eat this bread and drink the cup, you proclaim the Lord's death until He comes."

Supper/Communion/Eucharist is done, Christians are announcing Jesus' death while awaiting his return (1 Corinthians 11:26).

There are various ways throughout the branches of Christianity that Jesus' body and blood are remembered and there are significant theological differences related to what occurs to the elements (that is, the bread and wine). Some hold to the concept of the transubstantiation of the elements by which they literally turn into the body and blood of Jesus, whereas others see the elements as symbolic. Some substitute wine for grape juice. Some come forward to participate, while others remain in their seats. Some eat and drink of the elements more frequently than do others. I have participated in various modes of commemoration. Regardless of how it is specifically performed, it must be a solemn time of reflection to remember the very basis of the Christian faith. It is a time to contemplate the sacrificial death of Christ. It is also a time for self-examination to consider one's relationship with God and others. For me, I am reminded in that moment of the need to become more Christ-like.

Reflection Questions

1. How does your denomination or branch of Christianity practice the reenactment of Jesus' last meal and what is the theological view held by your congregation about the elements? If you are unsure about the theological stance, be sure to conduct some research or speak with someone about it.

2. Read over 1 Corinthians 11:23–34. What does it teach about preparing oneself to participate in commemorating Jesus' death?

3. Conducting studies into Jesus' death has enhanced my time of commemoration. How can some of the Scripture passages or discussions found in our studies be useful in your time of reflection the next time you take the elements?

35

Flesh and Blood
(Again)

And while they were eating, Jesus took *some* bread, and after a blessing, He broke *it* and gave *it* to the disciples, and said, "Take, eat; this is My body." And when He had taken a cup and given thanks, He gave *it* to them, saying, "Drink from it, all of you; for this is My blood of the covenant, which is poured out for many for forgiveness of sins."

—MATTHEW 26:26–28

The Gospel of Matthew shares with Mark, Luke, and 1 Corinthians the connection between Jesus' blood and the establishment of a new covenant, and it shares with Mark and Luke the notion of pouring out blood (*ekcheō*).[lvi] Matthew is unique, however, in its inclusion of Jesus' words that his blood was being poured with the purpose of obtaining forgiveness for the iniquities of many people. Both the ideas of covenant and Jesus' blood as a means of forgiveness relate to discussions in the book of Hebrews. There, the author utilizes the notion of providing an offering or sacrifice (*prospherō*) to describe the sacrificial death of Jesus as a definitive and single act of sacrifice through which Jesus provided his blood to secure cleansing from iniquity (Hebrews 9:14, 25, 28;[1] 10:12).[2] His blood was required due to the inadequacy of animal blood to remove sin (Hebrews 10:4)[3] and because of its inferior nature in contrast to Jesus' blood (Hebrews 9:23).[4] Jesus' blood, Hebrews explains, was the means by which a new covenant was established. In the Bible, both covenants and forgiveness necessitate shedding blood (Hebrews 9:18–22).[5] Hebrews 9:20, moreover, looks back to Moses' words in Exodus 24:8.[6] That passage is about the sealing of the Mosaic covenant through sprinkling the blood of animals (male calves) on the Israelites. Hebrews essentially teaches that just as the Mosaic Covenant required animal blood, the new covenant of Jesus Christ is built upon superior blood, that of the Savior. Matthew 26 parallels Hebrews and teaches that Jesus' blood established a new covenant, leading to forgiveness.

1. Hebrews 9:14, 25, and 28—"how much more will the blood of Christ, who through the eternal Spirit offered Himself without blemish to God, cleanse your conscience from dead works to serve the living God? . . . nor was it that He should offer Himself often, as the high priest enters the holy place year by year with blood not his own . . . so Christ also, having been offered once to bear the sins of many, shall appear a second time for salvation without *reference to* sin, to those who eagerly await Him."

2. Hebrews 10:12—"but He, having offered one sacrifice for sins for all time, sat down at the right hand of God."

3. Hebrews 10:4—"For it is impossible for the blood of bulls and goats to take away sins."

4. Hebrews 9:23—"Therefore it was necessary for the copies of the things in the heavens to be cleansed with these, but the heavenly things themselves with better sacrifices than these."

5. Hebrews 9:18–22—"Therefore even the first *covenant* was not inaugurated without blood. For when every commandment had been spoken by Moses to all the people according to the Law, he took the blood of the calves and the goats, with water and scarlet wool and hyssop, and sprinkled both the book itself and all the people, saying, 'This is the blood of the covenant which God commanded you.' And in the same way he sprinkled both the tabernacle and all the vessels of the ministry with the blood. And according to the Law, *one may* almost *say*, all things are cleansed with blood, and without shedding of blood there is no forgiveness."

6. Exodus 24:8—"So Moses took the blood and sprinkled *it* on the people, and said, 'Behold the blood of the covenant, which the Lord has made with you in accordance with all these words.'"

Covenants are at the core of God's relationships with people. I have often likened the idea of a covenant to a contractual agreement with obligations for both sides of the arrangement. When the Israelites accepted their contract at Sinai and were sprinkled with animal blood, they agreed to take on the obligations of keeping divine commandments (Exodus 24). The Israelites did so in exchange for divine promises. Hebrews chapter 8 explains that the promises undergirding the new covenant through Jesus are better than those from before. The chapter cites Jeremiah 31:31–34[7] to demonstrate the nature of the new covenant that came about because the Israelites did not keep the Mosaic Covenant. One of the key aspects of the new covenant is that God's teachings or laws will be placed into minds and written on hearts. In this new covenant, God will treat iniquity mercifully and forget sins. Thus, rather than an external set of laws and obligations, the new covenant relates to the internalization of divine principles. Such internalization will result in positive external responses. It is not that a series of obligations must be followed in order to receive divine approval, for that would be impossible as we have seen. Faith is the basis of entering into the new covenant, but it will spark an internal reaction to follow Godly ideals. The book of James speaks to the notion that a living faith produces external results (2:26).[8] Jesus is remembered for stating that producing fruit is a sign of true discipleship, and love is particularly emphasized in the passage (John 15).

---

7. Jeremiah 31:31–34—"'Behold, days are coming,' declares the Lord, 'when I will make a new covenant with the house of Israel and with the house of Judah, not like the covenant which I made with their fathers in the day I took them by the hand to bring them out of the land of Egypt, My covenant which they broke, although I was a husband to them,' declares the Lord. 'But this is the covenant which I will make with the house of Israel after those days,' declares the Lord, 'I will put My law within them, and on their heart I will write it; and I will be their God, and they shall be My people. And they shall not teach again, each man his neighbor and each man his brother, saying 'Know the Lord,' for they shall all know Me, from the least of them to the greatest of them,' declares the Lord, 'for I will forgive their iniquity, and their sin I will remember no more.'"

8. James 2:26—"For just as the body without *the* spirit is dead, so also faith without works is dead."

Reflection Questions

1. Read through Hebrews 10:1–18. According to the passage, why was it necessary for Jesus' sacrifice?

2. What is the importance of fruit in the life of a Christ-follower?

3. In today's passage, it states that Jesus' blood both established a covenant and resulted in cleansing from iniquity. In anticipation of tomorrow's study, is forgiveness from sin central to the Passover narrative? See Exodus 12:23–27 for assistance.

36

The Passover Lamb

Your boasting is not good. Do you not know that a little leaven leavens the whole lump *of dough*? Clean out the old leaven, that you may be a new lump, just as you are *in fact* unleavened. For Christ our Passover also has been sacrificed. Let us therefore celebrate the feast, not with old leaven, nor with the leaven of malice and wickedness, but with the unleavened bread of sincerity and truth.

—1 CORINTHIANS 5:6–8

knowing that you were not redeemed with perishable things like silver or gold from your futile way of life inherited from your forefathers, but with precious blood, as of a lamb unblemished and spotless, *the blood* of Christ.

—1 PETER 1:18–19

Passover is a fascinating time to be in Israel. Much must be done to prepare for the festival due to the presence of yeast products in the regular diet. Exodus 12:15[1] states that yeast or leaven must

---

1. Exodus 12:15—"Seven days you shall eat unleavened bread, but on the first day you shall remove leaven from your houses; for whoever eats anything leavened from the first day until the seventh day, that person shall be cut

be removed from homes and Deuteronomy 16:4[2] indicates that the Israelites could not be seen with yeast anywhere in their land during the holiday. Most noticeable to the modern general public is the eradication of yeast in the food industry. You can see in the modern supermarket, for instance, the cordoning off of a section of the store that contains yeast products. Large rolls of paper are used to cover shelves, thereby removing the offending foodstuffs from being accessible for consumption. The fast-food industry gets involved, too. I am admittedly disappointed that I never tried an American-styled burger served on matzah (unleavened bread) when in Jerusalem during Passover. It is a strange regret from my time in Israel, but it is not as odd as what a Jewish professor, whom I knew, encountered. He told me about how he dined on a pork sandwich on matzah served at a kibbutz that raised pigs. Such an item certainly is not kosher, despite its correspondence to Passover restrictions! His experience demonstrates that partial adherence does not count if a person is adhering to dietary laws. A bit of a restricted item can spoil the rest of the meal, as 1 Corinthians 5 explains.

The chapter from which the above quotation is taken concerns the effect of wrongful behavior infecting the believers at Corinth and the need to disassociate from Christians steeped in immoral practices. Passover is brought in to make a point about the leavening effects of sin—a bit of yeast, leavens the entire batch. For our purposes, the text is significant because of its clear equation of Jesus with Passover sacrifice. Rather than "our Passover," another translation renders the phrase as "our paschal lamb" (RSV). The Passover or Paschal lamb can be referred to in the Greek as *pascha* (Mark 14:12),[3] but that is also the word used for the holiday (Luke

---

off from Israel."

2. Deuteronomy 16:4—"For seven days no leaven shall be seen with you in all your territory, and none of the flesh which you sacrifice on the evening of the first day shall remain overnight until morning."

3. Mark 14:12—"And on the first day of Unleavened Bread, when the Passover *lamb* was being sacrificed, His disciples said to Him, 'Where do you want us to go and prepare for You to eat the Passover?'"

2:41[4]).[lvii] When we consider the pouring out of Jesus' blood at the time of Passover, we must be mindful that Passover is a festival that goes back to the concept of ransoming lives through lamb sacrifice and not to the notion of forgiveness of sin. Sacrifices such as guilt-offerings, sin-sacrifices, and Day of Atonement rituals were about removing sins. Hence, while Passover is important, other rites are significant when considering the sacrifice of Jesus, particularly as it relates to lamb sacrifice.

We previously discussed the connection between 1 Peter 1:18–19[5] and Passover; not only does the passage correspond to the idea of ransoming, but it explains that the redemption is secured through Jesus' blood, which is like a pure lamb's blood. The same word for lamb in 1 Peter 1:18–19 (*amnos*) appears at the beginning of John's Gospel where John the Baptist is noted for his exclamation that Jesus was "the Lamb of God who takes away the sin of the world" (1:29)—such an idea of Jesus carrying off sin (*airō*)[lviii] is paralleled in 1 John 3:5.[6] In John 1:29, the lamb (*amnos*) is not specifically designated as a Passover lamb. That by itself would not exclude the verse from alluding to Passover sacrifice. The concept of taking away sin, however, does show that the Passover lamb was not the intended focus of John 1. Lambs were used in the sacrificial system for rites, such as daily sacrifices (Exodus 29:38)[7] and guilt sacrifices (Numbers 6:12).[8] The performance of sacrifices for guilt, known as guilt offerings, is a

---

4. Luke 2:41—"And His parents used to go to Jerusalem every year at the Feast of the Passover."

5. 1 Peter 1:18–19—"knowing that you were not redeemed with perishable things like silver or gold from your futile way of life inherited from your forefathers, but with precious blood, as of a lamb unblemished and spotless, *the blood* of Christ."

6. 1 John 3:5—"And you know that He appeared in order to take away sins; and in Him there is no sin."

7. Exodus 29:38—"Now this is what you shall offer on the altar: two one year old lambs each day, continuously."

8. Numbers 6:12—"and shall dedicate to the Lord his days as a Nazirite, and shall bring a male lamb a year old for a guilt offering; but the former days shall be void because his separation was defiled."

particularly important practice related to the sacrificial death of Jesus. Isaiah 53 specifically describes such a sacrifice and the early church recognized the connection between that chapter and Jesus' death. Sometimes it takes the help of a stranger to understand the connection, as an Ethiopian eunuch once learned. We will meet him tomorrow.

Reflection Questions

1. How is Passover significant for the interpretation of Jesus' sacrificial death?

2. To what extent does Passover sufficiently reflect the various aspects of Jesus' sacrificial death as presented in the New Testament?

3. What are some of the leavening elements in our lives that need to be removed?

37

Reading Isaiah

And he arose and went; and behold, there was an Ethiopian eunuch, a court official of Candace, queen of the Ethiopians, who was in charge of all her treasure; and he had come to Jerusalem to worship. And he was returning and sitting in his chariot, and was reading the prophet Isaiah. And the Spirit said to Philip, "Go up and join this chariot." And when Philip had run up, he heard him reading Isaiah the prophet, and said, "Do you understand what you are reading?" And he said, "Well, how could I, unless someone guides me?" And he invited Philip to come up and sit with him.

—ACTS 8:27-31

Acts 8 indicates that as Philip was on his way to Jerusalem from preaching in Samaria, he was told by an angel to go to the other side of Jerusalem and proceed along the road, heading towards Gaza. This would have been a thoroughfare for people traveling from Jerusalem on their way to Egypt and other African destinations. On the road, he encountered an Ethiopian official, but not just any member of the royal entourage. He was a eunuch and that is how he is remembered, not by his name.

Why would his physical status be important to the narrative? As a eunuch, he constituted a type of person, who, according to the book of Deuteronomy (23:1),[1] was unworthy to gather in God's assembly. As such a person, he may have been particularly interested in a passage from the scroll of Isaiah that speaks about eunuchs and foreigners. The text indicates such things as eunuchs being granted a name and memorial in the Temple that exceeds the posterity of children, and the passage speaks about foreigners coming to participate in Temple worship (Isaiah 56). As a foreigner and a eunuch who believed in the God of Israel and was in Jerusalem to worship, I assume that the book of Isaiah would have been of significance to him.

The Ethiopian official would have been holding a scroll, which was how the book of Isaiah was recorded in those days. This would have been a very expensive text to own and I wonder if he recently purchased it while in Jerusalem on behalf of his queen. In general, most people would neither have easy access to a copy of a biblical book nor would many be able to read it. Reading while being jostled along in a chariot must not have been a simple task. There are certainly several unique aspects about this narrative.

At the time that Philip caught up with the Ethiopian man, he was close to the section of Isaiah about eunuchs. The eunuch was reading from the part of Isaiah related to the Suffering Servant and was specifically at Isaiah 53:7-8,[2] which speaks about the killing of one who is quiet like a silent sheep on its way to be slaughtered and a silent lamb (*amnos*) in the presence of the shearer. The Ethiopian was curious about the person mentioned in the passage. Philip used Isaiah as a starting point to explain that Jesus of Nazareth was the focal point of Isaiah 52-53, likely mentioning how he was very quiet in the midst of the accusations leveled at him prior

1. Deuteronomy 23:1—"No one who is emasculated, or has his male organ cut off, shall enter the assembly of the Lord."

2. Isaiah 53:7-8—"He was oppressed and He was afflicted, yet He did not open His mouth; like a lamb that is led to slaughter, and like a sheep that is silent before its shearers, so He did not open His mouth. By oppression and judgment He was taken away; and as for His generation, who considered that He was cut off out of the land of the living, for the transgression of my people to whom the stroke *was due?*"

to his execution. The Ethiopian responded with faith, accepting the message, believing in Jesus, and receiving baptism immediately.

While there is no indication that Philip went into detail about another part of the passage that corresponds to the relationship between a lamb, Isaiah 52-53, and Jesus, a few verses past where the Ethiopian was reading there is a reference that connects the Suffering Servant to the concept of a guilt offering (53:10).[3] A guilt offering was a sacrifice that could be accomplished with a ram, resulting in atonement and forgiveness (Leviticus 5:17-19).[4]

There are additional references to the Suffering Servant and addressing sin, and we shall continue discussing the passage tomorrow. I wish to conclude by indicating that Isaiah 52-53 is an extremely rare text of Scripture in comparison to anything else found in the Hebrew Bible. It has no rival in terms of the way that it conveys the idea of a human functioning as a substitutionary sacrifice for the sins of others. We already considered a passage that comes close, but Micah 6 only questions the idea of sacrificing an individual to address the sins of another person. The only innocent vicarious victims endorsed in the Hebrew Bible in terms of addressing iniquity are animals, that is, with the exception of the human substitutionary victim of Isaiah 52-53.

Reflection Questions

1. Isaiah 56 (a passage mentioning eunuchs and foreigners) was about God including the excluded in worship.

---

3. Isaiah 53:10—"But the Lord was pleased to crush Him, putting *Him* to grief; if He would render Himself *as* a guilt offering, He will see *His* offspring, He will prolong *His* days, and the good pleasure of the Lord will prosper in His hand."

4. Leviticus 5:17-19—"Now if a person sins and does any of the things which the Lord has commanded not to be done, though he was unaware, still he is guilty, and shall bear his punishment. He is then to bring to the priest a ram without defect from the flock, according to your valuation, for a guilt offering. So the priest shall make atonement for him concerning his error in which he sinned unintentionally and did not know *it*, and it shall be forgiven him. It is a guilt offering; he was certainly guilty before the Lord."

What is the broader context of the Ethiopian's encounter with Philip as recorded in Acts 8, and how does the chapter demonstrate the inclusive nature of Jesus' message? How should it remind us to be inclusive?

2. Read through Isaiah 52:13–53:12. How often and how is sin mentioned in the chapter?

3. How does Isaiah 52-53 further our understanding of Jesus as the Lamb of God?

38

Both the Lamb and the Shepherd

For you have been called for this purpose, since Christ also suffered for you, leaving you an example for you to follow in His steps, who committed no sin, nor was any deceit found in His mouth; and while being reviled, He did not revile in return; while suffering, He uttered no threats, but kept entrusting *Himself* to Him who judges righteously; and He Himself bore our sins in His body on the cross, that we might die to sin and live to righteousness; for by His wounds you were healed. For you were continually straying like sheep, but now you have returned to the Shepherd and Guardian of your souls.

—1 PETER 2:21-25

These words appear in the context of a discussion about unjust suffering and the way to respond to it. Christians are told to follow the model established by Jesus, who reacted to his own wrongful suffering without responding inappropriately. He lived out the idea of patient endurance in the face of being harmed for doing what was right. Jesus, the passage explains, went so far as to carry bodily the sins of others in the crucifixion even though he was himself sinless—this is the essence of injustice: dying for a transgression that you did not commit. The purpose of Jesus' bearing of iniquity was that people might exist as dead to sin but alive to righteousness. Thus, in these few verses, there appears a profound examination of the sacrificial death of Christ that was introduced mainly to present an example for how to handle injustice.

In representing the sacrifice of Jesus, Isaiah 52-53 is woven into the narrative seamlessly. There are four instances of direct quotations from or allusions to Isaiah 52-53 in 1 Peter 2:23–25. The following phrases from the above quotation relate to Isaiah 53:4, 5, 6, 9, 11 and 12: "who committed no sin, nor was any deceit found in His mouth"; "bore our sins"; "by His wounds you were healed"; and "straying like sheep." The notion of bearing our sins is especially worthy of our attention. Isaiah 53:4, 11, and 12[1] are noteworthy in terms of substitutional suffering through carrying the iniquities of others, and one key emphasis of Isaiah 52-53 is upon the crushing weight of people's sins upon the shoulders of the Suffering Servant. Hebrews 9:28 seems to draw upon Isaiah 53, too, specifically 53:12, when it states: "so Christ also, having been offered once to bear the sins of many."

It goes against our human nature to stand idly by when accused of something we did not do, and we certainly do not feel inclined to accept the punishment rightly deserved by others. In fact, generally we are not willing to accept the punishment we rightly deserve. We seek out mercy by which our rightful punishment will not be applied to us. Titus 3:5[2] speaks to this when it explains that mercy is the basis of salvation; and Isaiah 53:5[3] explains that the Suffering Servant bore the punishment for our well-being.

1. Isaiah 53:4, 11, and 12—"Surely our griefs He Himself bore, and our sorrows He carried; yet we ourselves esteemed Him stricken, smitten of God, and afflicted . . . As a result of the anguish of His soul, He will see *it* and be satisfied; by His knowledge the Righteous One, My Servant, will justify the many, as He will bear their iniquities. Therefore, I will allot Him a portion with the great, and He will divide the booty with the strong; because He poured out Himself to death, and was numbered with the transgressors; yet He Himself bore the sin of many, and interceded for the transgressors."

2. Titus 3:5—"He saved us, not on the basis of deeds which we have done in righteousness, but according to His mercy, by the washing of regeneration and renewing by the Holy Spirit."

3. Isaiah 53:5—"But He was pierced through for our transgressions, He was crushed for our iniquities; the chastening for our well-being *fell* upon Him, and by His scourging we are healed."

Considering these two verses together, makes me think about God's mercy and grace—not only do we avoid the condemnation that we merit, but we also receive God's favor and blessings through the suffering of the Messiah.

We sin. He was punished unfairly. We are forgiven. We are made whole.

Reflection Questions

1. How does 2 Corinthians 5:20–21 relate to today's discussion of Isaiah 52-53 and 1 Peter 2?

2. How does 1 Peter 2 utilize the sacrificial death of Jesus to encourage the reader?

3. What encourages you from today's study?

39

The Mercy Seat

But now apart from the Law *the* righteousness of God has been
manifested, being witnessed by the Law and the Prophets, even *the*
righteousness of God through faith in Jesus Christ for all those who
believe; for there is no distinction; for all have sinned and fall short
of the glory of God, being justified as a gift by His grace through the
redemption which is in Christ Jesus; whom God displayed publicly
as a propitiation in His blood through faith. *This was* to demonstrate His righteousness, because in the forbearance of God He
passed over the sins previously committed; for the demonstration,
I say, of His righteousness at the present time, that He might be just
and the justifier of the one who has faith in Jesus.

—ROMANS 3:21–26

From the standpoint of popular culture, the Ark of the Covenant
is the most fascinating furnishing of the Tabernacle/Temple.
As an historian, it occasionally enters into discussions I am having
with students. Admittedly I have not spent an extensive amount of
time thinking about what happened to it, but I once had a border
guard express to me his perspective on where the Ark once resided.
As my car sat, awaiting clearance to pass, the guard explained that
at the time of Jesus' death, the Ark of the Covenant was located in
a subterranean chamber below the place of the crucifixion so that

Jesus' blood could drip down onto the Ark. I am unsure of the evidence for such a claim and ever since hearing it, I have doubted its historical accuracy. Still, I can understand why such a view would be asserted: the Ark of the Covenant was central to the Day of Atonement. The high priest would bring the sacrificial blood from sin offerings into the Holy of Holies and apply the blood of a bull and a goat to the mercy seat that was part of the Ark (Leviticus 16). Going behind the veil or curtain separating the holiest section of the Tabernacle/Temple would have been the most hallowed and harrowing part of the day. Entering there was regarded as entering into God's presence. It was not something to be taken lightly.

Not wishing to argue with my new acquaintance, the border guard and I parted on friendly terms and my wife and I resumed our trip back from Montreal without any issues. Had the writer of Hebrews been speaking to the guard instead of me, the conversation would likely have taken a different turn given that Hebrews 9 diminishes the significance of *earthly* Tabernacle features in promoting the idea that Jesus, as high priest, came into the *heavenly* Holy of Holies by means of his blood. The earthly Ark would have been of limited importance for the writer of Hebrews—the earthly replicas of the things in heaven and the entire sacrificial system became obsolete through the sacrifice of Jesus. There was no longer a need for animal sacrifice, for instance.

As already noted, part of the Ark was the mercy seat. Romans 3:25 uses the idea of the mercy seat (*hilastērion*)[lix] in conjunction with Jesus. There are at least three ways that translations have chosen to understand this verse: the first is to translate the word as reflecting propitiation or expiation (ASV, CSB, ESV, RSV, KJV, NASB); the second is to designate it as a sacrifice that brings about atonement (NIV, NRSV); and the third is to render it as mercy seat (Darby, Tyndale, Young's Literal, CEB). The latter is how the word (*hilastērion*) generally occurs in the Greek version of the Hebrew Bible (Exodus 25:17),[1] and it relates to a physical object. The other two options are more abstract. Romans 3:25 is best explained

1. Exodus 25:17—"And you shall make a mercy seat of pure gold, two and a half cubits long and one and a half cubits wide."

by the more abstract idea because a literal mercy seat does not seem to be the intention. What is perhaps going on here is that one of the objects associated with atonement came to represent the concept of atonement. Something similar happened in terms of Jesus' cross, which has taken on symbolic meaning beyond the physical object (see Philippians 3:18).[2] Thus, Romans 3:25 can be regarded to mean that Jesus was a victim of sacrifice by which atonement/expiation was secured.

Atonement fits into the broader passage because the text is about how a person (Jew or non-Jew) becomes morally and judiciously correct (justified) in God's eyes. It is not by following the Law, but by faith in Jesus. Attempting to obtain a correct status before God by keeping biblical principles fails. We need to stop trying. Today's passage states that "all have sinned and fall short of the glory of God." Faith in the atoning work of Jesus results in an upright status, and through the work of sanctification, our faith produces thoughts and actions that are virtuous.

Reflection Questions

1. How does today's passage add another feature to our understanding of the ways that biblical writers described the sacrificial death of Jesus?

2. How does today's passage, including verses 27–31, conform to ideas already discussed, such as faith versus the Law, grace, and blood?

3. Which of the three translation options listed above for mercy seat (*hilastērion*) is used in your favorite translation of Romans 3:25 and which option makes the best sense to you? Why?

---

2. Philippians 3:18—"For many walk, of whom I often told you, and now tell you even weeping, *that they are* enemies of the cross of Christ."

40

Beyond the Veil

And Jesus uttered a loud cry, and breathed His last. And the veil of the temple was torn in two from top to bottom. And when the centurion, who was standing right in front of Him, saw the way He breathed His last, he said, "Truly this man was the Son of God!"

—MARK 15:37–39

Since therefore, brethren, we have confidence to enter the holy place by the blood of Jesus, by a new and living way which He inaugurated for us through the veil, that is, His flesh, and since *we have* a great priest over the house of God, let us draw near with a sincere heart in full assurance of faith, having our hearts sprinkled *clean* from an evil conscience and our bodies washed with pure water.

—HEBREWS 10:19–22

In Hebrews 9 the earthly Tabernacle and the rites performed there are compared to the heavenly sanctuary. The chapter argues that the blood of Jesus was better than the blood of animals, for the high priest on earth goes into the Holy of Holies one time a year through the use of animal blood, whereas Christ went into the inner part of the Tabernacle in heaven through his own blood, obtaining for all time the elimination of iniquity by means of sacrificing himself. A veil cut off the innermost part of the Tabernacle from the adjacent chamber. According to the Gospels (Matthew 27:51),[1] the veil ripped apart in conjunction with Jesus' crucifixion.[ix] This symbolically represents that the way into the Holy of Holies was opened up, providing greater accessibility to God. The book of Hebrews similarly addresses the idea to explain that the followers of Christ are given access past the veil, indicating that Jesus served as a forerunner for entering (6:19–20).[2] Christians may move into the inner space due to Jesus' blood (10:19–20). Unlike the earthly veil, Hebrews designates that the curtain constitutes Jesus' flesh. The body of Jesus serves as a barrier that requires crossing so that one is able to come into God's presence. What is more, God can only be approached by means of the cleansing effects of Christ's shed blood. In the quotation from Hebrews 10 provided above, we are encouraged to come into this presence with confidence. Hebrews 4:14–16 has this to add to the discussion:

> Since then we have a great high priest who has passed through the heavens, Jesus the Son of God, let us hold fast our confession. For we do not have a high priest who cannot sympathize with our weaknesses, but One who has been tempted in all things as *we are, yet* without sin. Let us therefore draw near with confidence to the throne of grace, that we may receive mercy and may find grace to help in time of need.

What a blessing to approach God directly because we have been purified through the atoning work of our high priest (Hebrews

---

1. Matthew 27:51—"And behold, the veil of the temple was torn in two from top to bottom, and the earth shook; and the rocks were split" (see Mark 15:38; Luke 23:45).

2. Hebrews 6:19-20—"This hope we have as an anchor of the soul, a *hope* both sure and steadfast and one which enters within the veil, where Jesus has entered as a forerunner for us, having become a high priest forever according to the order of Melchizedek."

2:17).[3] Jesus is both the one who performed the sacrifice (high priest) and the victim of sacrifice. Jesus' blood is of paramount importance to the Christian faith. To demonstrate this significance, Hebrews uses three different bloody rites from the Israelite tradition. While Hebrews references such things as covenantal bloodletting and the use of heifer's ashes, which contained burned blood, for purification purposes (Hebrews 9), the Day of Atonement or Yom Kippur was particularly important to the writer of Hebrews. This is seen in the above quotation from Hebrews 10. We have encountered Yom Kippur in a previous discussion, such as in reference to Hebrews 13:11–12.[4] There, Hebrews explains that the crucifixion occurred outside the city gate in parallel to what was done outside the Israelite camp on the Day of Atonement. It was there that the bull and goat, whose shed blood facilitated atonement on Yom Kippur, were set on fire (Leviticus 16:27).[5]

Reflection Questions

1. To what extent do we take access to God for granted and how should the passages encountered in today's study prompt us to respond to the ease by which Christians can pass behind the veil?

2. If Jesus died during Passover, why is the Day of Atonement important to the sacrificial understanding of Jesus' death?

3. Hebrews 2:17—"Therefore, He had to be made like His brethren in all things, that He might become a merciful and faithful high priest in things pertaining to God, to make propitiation for the sins of the people."

4. Hebrews 13:11–12—"For the bodies of those animals whose blood is brought into the holy place by the high priest *as an offering* for sin, are burned outside the camp. Therefore Jesus also, that He might sanctify the people through His own blood, suffered outside the gate."

5. Leviticus 16:27—"But the bull of the sin offering and the goat of the sin offering, whose blood was brought in to make atonement in the holy place, shall be taken outside the camp, and they shall burn their hides, their flesh, and their refuse in the fire."

3. Read through one of the crucifixion narratives, such as Mark 15. The centurion, who stood near the cross, was particularly impacted by the manner in which Jesus died. What response does it cause in you?

Conclusion

How does one end forty days of reflection upon the foundational event of Christianity? We should begin by stating that Jesus' death, while of great significance, is only part of the story. It is an essential part to be sure, but there is more, for "if Christ has not been raised, your faith is worthless; you are still in your sins . . . But now Christ has been raised from the dead, the first fruits of those who are asleep." (1 Corinthians 15:17, 20). The resurrection is as central to the faith as the sacrificial death. Good Friday is a solemn day, remembering the sufferings of the cross. Easter or Resurrection Sunday is a more joyous affair, celebrating life and the empty tomb. Every baptism, as we have seen, is a way of identifying the Christ follower with the death, burial, and resurrection of Jesus. We need not reserve our celebration of the resurrection for one day in spring every year. Every sunrise can remind us of the resurrection of Christ and the newness of spiritual life bestowed upon the believer. Putting both together by gathering at sunrise on Easter is a special time of commemoration, especially when baptisms are involved.

We can also end by summarizing some of the key concepts that we have encountered. As you may have noticed, we only scratched the surface. More can and has been written on issues and passages addressed here. Simply stated, the forty studies were about how the sacrificial death of Jesus was represented in the New Testament in light of the Israelite ritual and textual traditions. The studies also showed how this death should be emulated on a daily basis. Essential to our study was the idea of blood. Blood, as we have seen, is vital. In fact, it is the very essence of life and vitality. The Israelites understood that life is contained in the blood. I was mindful of blood's importance as I wrote some of the words of this paragraph as Alexander was next to me attached to a unit of blood by means of an IV because of low iron in his bloodstream. Someone, somewhere kindly donated their blood, not knowing how it would be used specifically. This person helped restore vitality and strength to Alexander. As parents, Krista and I were faced with two options: to accept a blood transfusion or to wait weeks for his health to improve through supplements. The transfusion promised more instantaneous results and we were concerned about the physical effect the slower process would have on Alexander's heart, which had been working extra hard. We chose the shorter route to improved health through the medical advice we received and prayerfully considering the options. Even as he was only partially through the process, his heart rate improved; he became stronger through receiving blood. There is a parallel to be noted here between the life-giving power of Jesus' blood and modern medical transfusions. Alexander recognized the similarity as we drove home from the hospital, but transfusions pale dramatically in comparison because there is no sacrifice, no cleansing effect, no justification, no sanctification, no redemption—in short, no spiritual power. Transfusions assist in physical life, but they go no farther.

We encountered a variety of rituals, most of them bloody, which were used in the New Testament to explain the sacrificial death of Christ. The Day of Atonement was of particular significance, as was Passover, guilt offerings, covenantal bloodletting, bronze serpent elevation, and firstborn sacrifice. All members of the Trinity were active in the sacrifice, but the biblical texts primarily emphasize the role of the Father in sacrificing his son and the Son's participation in the ritual as both the one sacrificing and the victim. The biblical writers did not limit themselves to a single ritual or historical narrative to explain the substitutionary suffering of Jesus. The sacrificial death of Jesus and its results are important, though complex.

We can also conclude with an eye towards moving forward. How this will look for each of us will vary. The texts we have engaged and the God we have encountered will spur us on into actions and words that impact our personal lives and relationships. We are, like the early church, "always carrying about in the body the dying of Jesus, that the life of Jesus also may be manifested in our body" (2 Corinthians 4:10). The death and life of Christ are integral aspects of who we are. The more we yield to the Holy Spirit and the work of sanctification in our lives, the more we will reflect Jesus in what we think, say, and do. We will tell others of this work. We will serve more selflessly. We will live more sacrificially as we more completely live not in the old self with its iniquitous practices and selfishness, but in the new self that is being more and more renewed into the image of God and less and less conformed to earthly ways. In this process, we will better love God and others, thereby embodying the essence of the earlier covenant, not because we are required to fulfill the Law, but due to our transformation through the later covenant ushered in by the blood of the slain Lamb of God who is worthy "to receive power and riches and wisdom and might and honor and glory and blessing" (Revelation 5:12).

Endnotes

i.   Based upon Hebrew usage in light of its ancient Near Eastern context, the Israelites regarded atonement as a purifying process; see Milgrom, *Leviticus*, 1079–84; Gilders, *Blood Ritual in the Hebrew Bible*, 28–29; Geyer, "Blood and the Nations," 1–20; and Levine, *In the Presence of the Lord*, 55–77 and 123–27.

ii.   The New Testament was originally written in Greek, a popular language of the ancient world stemming from the conquests of the Greek ruler, Alexander the Great. Prior to the creation of the New Testament, the Hebrew Bible (or Old Testament) was translated into Greek. This Greek version of the early Scriptures is called the Septuagint. Scholars can compare the Hebrew or Aramaic of the Hebrew Bible to the Greek of the Septuagint in order to appreciate how passages were perceived and interpreted. I wish to note that the treatment of the biblical texts in Hebrew and Greek that is provided in this book was enhanced by the access I had to the BibleWorks software system and the analytical resources contained therein. Searching the ancient languages was conducted with relative ease through this resource. Lexical resources in book form were also consulted and relevant citations have been provided.

iii.   For more on the Greek behind the idea of "giving" in John 3:16, which is represented by the word *didōmi*, see Danker, *A Greek-English Lexicon*, 242–43.

iv.   The Hebrew word (*ḥesed*) translated here as "kindness/steadfast love" is not consistently rendered into English by a single idea. The RSV, for instance, translates it as "kindness" in Micah 6:8, but as "steadfast love" in Micah 7:18. The NASB similarly renders it as "kindness" and "unchanging love" in those verses. The concept of an unchanging, steadfast, or even faithful love may best reflect the Hebrew usage because the word is coupled at times with the notion of faithfulness (Hebrew *ʾemet*), as in Micah 7:20 (see Proverbs 3:3; 20:28) where *ḥesed* parallels *ʾemet*. The NASB translates the latter as "truth" in Mic 7:20, but notes that "faithfulness" is a viable option. A professor of mine in graduate school (Brian B. Schmidt) encouraged us to translate it as "loyal love."

v.   This brief translation is my own.

vi.   This is but one of the prophetic passages that emphasizes non-sacri-
         ficial pursuits above ritual practices (see also 2 Samuel 15 or Isaiah
         58).

vii.   This translation is my own.

viii.   My friend, David Allgire, preached a sermon at Compassion Chris-
         tian Church (July 20, 2014) that encouraged me to return to John
         3:16 and to give it further consideration in comparison to Genesis
         22. His interpretation of John 3:16 is that it represents Jesus in paral-
         lel to Isaac. The two passages are certainly intertwined.

ix.   Technically, Isaac was Abraham's second son; Ishmael being the first.
         Isaac, however, was regarded as the legitimate heir through Sarah.
         The reference to Isaac being loved may have been included to indi-
         cate the preference given to Isaac over Ishmael.

x.   The Greek provides *hilasmos* for Hebrew ideas about forgiveness
         (Psalm 129:4 [Greek 130:4]), sin-offering (Ezekiel 44:27), and
         atonement (Leviticus 25:9).

xi.   The word translated as "Advocate" is *paraklētos*, which appears in
         the New Testament solely in 1 John and the book of John. The word
         was employed variously in the ancient world, but it did serve to des-
         ignate a person who provided assistance in court. Such is the sense
         of the word in the current passage under consideration. See Behm
         in Bromiley, *Theological Dictionary*, 782–83.

xii.   Here, I am following in part the lexical analyses of Friberg et al.,
         Analytical Lexicon, #21619; and Lust et al., *Greek-English Lexicon*,
         #5617.

xiii.   Like John 3:16, the Greek word *didōmi* is employed to indicate the
         notion of giving.

xiv.   See the online presentation at Szymanski, "Reading the Text."

xv.   Here, I am taking the verb as reflecting a sacrificial idea in a man-
         ner similar to *didōmi* in John 3:16. For the use of *paradidōmi* in a
         clear sacrificial context, consider the Greek of Isaiah 53:6, 12. On
         the basic meaning of "to give over/up," see Danker, *A Greek–English
         Lexicon*, 76–63.

xvi.   The Mishnah and Talmud are premodern Jewish books of law,
         recording discussions held by various rabbis. They represent an
         important phase in the development of Judaism after the Second
         Temple was destroyed by Rome in AD 70. Early rabbinical teachings
         are considered to form the Oral Torah (Law), complementing the

Torah (Law), written in the first five books of the Bible.

xvii. As one Greek lexicon similarly explains in relation to the New Testament word for condemnation (*katakrima*) and associated words that "'condemnation' does not denote merely a pronouncement of guilt . . . but the adjudication of punishment." Danker, *A Greek-English Lexicon*, 518.

xviii. The lexical discussion provided here aligns with Lust et al., *Greek-English Lexicon*, #457; Danker, *A Greek-English Lexicon*, 51.

xix. The cross-reference of the NASB correctly identifies Psalm 40:6 as the verse from which the quotation in Hebrews 10:6 was drawn. The Greek of Psalm 40:6 has a different verb than in Hebrews 10:6, but the construction of "for sin" is the same.

xx. The Hebrew of Leviticus 16:3 has a similar construction inasmuch as "for sin" could also be translated as a reference to a sin-sacrifice. Whether "for sin" should be regarded as a reference to a form of sacrifice depends upon the context. In Romans 8, the context allows for either "for a sin-sacrifice" or "for sin." The purpose of sending Jesus in either understanding still relates to the notion that he was sent to address sin.

xxi. In terms of focusing the mind upon the spirit (8:5–6), the word can refer to an individual's spirit or to God's Spirit. The general emphasis of the chapter is upon the latter, making it acceptable to view most of the references to spirit in Romans 8 as indicating the Holy Spirit, as the NASB has done.

xxii. Translation mine with correspondence to the wording of the NASB, taking into account the sacrificial nuance of *paradōmi* and an alternative translation of *charizomai*. On the varied meaning of *charizomai*, including its relation to forgiveness, see Danker, *A Greek-English Lexicon*, 1078.

xxiii. Hebrews 7:25 speaks about Jesus as an intercessor in a different context, that of his role as high priest.

xxiv. In Romans 5:16, "justification" is employed as the translation for a Greek word (*dikaiōma*), but the same word is translated as "act of righteousness" in verse 18. This demonstrates that the translators of the NASB recognized that biblical justification is linked to righteousness, but the Greek word can also be translated as "requirement" (Romans 8:4; NASB). Confusing, right? To simplify matters, it is acceptable to translate the word in all three ways. Schrenk in Bromiley, *Theological Dictionary*, 176. The "justification" at the end of Romans 5:18 is given for *dikaiōsis*, which, in addition to "justification," can also mean "acquittal" or "vindication." So Danker, *A*

Greek-English Lexicon, 250.

xxv. The NASB translation only has "justification" three times in the entire Bible and they are all in the New Testament. The words translated as such are mentioned in the previous footnote.

xxvi. So Schrenk in Bromiley, *Theological Dictionary*, 175.

xxvii. Both Romans 4 and Galatians 3 refer to righteousness or *dikaiosunē*. One Greek dictionary notes that the word corresponds generally to uprightness, but that in the New Testament things are more complex, identifying three areas of use: (1) judicial responsibly, as in justice; (2) judicial correctness in the context of redemption, as in righteousness; and (3) behavioral uprightness, as in righteousness and uprightness. There is also the word translated as righteous (*dikaios*) in verses like Romans 5:7 and 19. The word can denote moral excellence as in being upright or just, and can indicate what is right or fair in fulfilling justice. Danker, *A Greek-English Lexicon*, 246–48. Thus, both righteousness and righteous can relate to notions of justice and moral uprightness. My sense of a text like Romans 5 is that the justified person is both morally and judicially upright. Admittedly, my view is influenced in part by the lexical discussions in Danker and Bromily (see, for instance, the various citations in this and other footnotes for today's study).

xxviii. The chapter explains that righteousness is a gift—it is obtained through justification.

xxix. Justification is represented here as a process or as something that will be accomplished at a later date.

xxx. Notice that in Galatians 2:16–21 we can posit a functional definition of justification, that is, to be justified by faith relates to gaining righteousness. The parallel is that we neither gain justification nor righteousness through the Law but through faith (compare verses 16 and 21). Such is the focus of Galatians 3.

xxxi. 1 John 3:16 is not explicitly sacrificial, but it indicates that Jesus' death demonstrates what constitutes love and Christians should follow in his footsteps to give up their lives for the sake of other Christians.

xxxii. The analysis of *hagiazō* relates very well to the views expressed in Danker, *A Greek-English Lexicon*, 10, on the nature of the verb.

xxxiii. Hebrews 2:11 uses a similar participial form as in 10:14 to indicate that people are being made holy; yet, the *ESV* renders the relevant part of Hebrews 2:11 as "who are sanctified" instead of the "who are being sanctified" of 10:14. The latter translation is viable for both verses. We could argue that a process of being made holy is evident in both verses. In writing about Hebrews 10:14, Robertson said of the participle that its form is "either because of the process still going on or because of the repetition in so many persons as in 2:11." *Word Pictures*, 409. Regarding Hebrews 2:11, he stated: "It is a process here as in 10:14, not a single act, though 10:10 the perfect passive indicative presents a completed state." *Word Pictures*, 348. My sense that sanctification is presented in Hebrews as both a process and an imparted status was confirmed when I turned to Robertson's work. Previously, my thoughts on positional versus physical status were influenced by the introduction classes (called Next Steps) at my local congregation (Compassion Christian Church), which I helped facilitate occasionally. The guidebook from which we taught had a section focusing on the difference between positional status and the process of maturing in Christ. While complicated, both concepts are important in New Testament theology.

xxxiv.   This treatment aligns with the discussion in Danker, *A Greek-English Lexicon*, 10–11.

xxxv.   The verb translated as "to serve" in the quotation of Hebrews 9:14 is *latreuō*, which could be used in the Greek Septuagint to designate things done in a sacrificial sense, as well as to indicate moral and religious behavior. The cultic focus of the word is the more typical use. The New Testament employs the word similarly, but emphasizes more spiritualized service rather than literal sacrificial ministry. Strathmann in Bromiley, *Theological Dictionary*, 503–504.

xxxvi.   The word behind what the NASB translated as "sharing" has been recognized as a reference in Hebrews 13:16 to the idea of looking after those in need, specifically impoverished Christians. Wuest, *Word Studies*, 239.

xxxvii. While it is not Jesus who stated it, it is intriguing to read the dialogue between Jesus and a scribe on the issue of the two greatest commandments. The scribe affirmed Jesus' identification of their importance and added that sacrificial practices are less important (Mark 12:28–34). Regarding Jesus' words on things more important than rituals, his treatment of keeping Sabbath practices comes to mind (Matthew 12:1–13).

xxxviii. In light of the use of *eleos* for Hebrew *ḥesed* (as in Micah 6), I appreciate the treatment of *eleos* by Bultmann in Bromiley, *Theological Dictionary*, 222–23. He recognized that the Hebrew word is normally rendered as *eleos* in the Greek. In his discussion of the New Testament, he considered *eleos* as indicative of "gracious faithfulness" by God. This provides a different dimension to what we normally consider as "mercy."

xxxix.	Wuest, *Word Studies*, 239.
xl.	Another verse to consider in the area of sacrificial giving is Philippians 4:18.
xli.	My comments correlate to the treatment in Danker, *A Greek-English Lexicon*, 27, which includes other verses of relevance.
xlii.	I prefer the ESV over the NASB in terms of the verse's idea that God is to be praised in conjunction with the acknowledgment of his name, rather than in conjunction with thanksgiving. God certainly deserves gratitude, but the sense of the verse is better rendered by the notion of acknowledgement.
xliii.	On the sacrificial and non-sacrificial usage of the verb, see Danker, *A Greek-English Lexicon*, 886.
xliv.	The price is Jesus' blood. Revelation 5:9 indicates that the blood of the lamb (or Jesus) was the means of purchasing (*agorazō*) people unto God. The same verb for purchasing is found in 1 Corinthians 6:20.
xlv.	Revelation 1:5 speaks to the work of Jesus' blood in providing release from iniquity; and Ephesians 1:7 indicates that in Jesus there is redemption due to his blood, as well as forgiveness.
xlvi.	Firstborn donkeys were also redeemable animals (Exodus 13:13). They were not regarded as sacrificial animals. Firstborn animals that were dedicated to God were to be sacrificed.
xlvii.	While lambs are typically regarded as the sacrificial victims of Passover, goats were acceptable (Exodus 12:5).
xlviii.	First Peter 1:18–19 is paralleled by Titus 2:14 regarding redemption (see my chapters 6 and 7) and by 2 Peter 3:14 concerning the concept of blameless and spotless.
xlix.	The word *paristēmi* connotes nearness (Luke 1:19), including the idea of presenting a person or something to someone else (Acts 23:33). There are instances in which the verb can indicate dedication (see Luke 2:22), which is the way that I have taken Romans 12:1. While my perspective partially overlaps with that found in Danker, *A Greek-English Lexicon*, 778, I would not regard the word as a technical sacrificial verb.
l.	"Service" is an accepted translation of *latreia*, but it is important to note that the word is intertwined with ritual performance at a cultic spot, including sacrificial behavior like Passover (see Exodus

12:25–27). In New Testament usage, the sacrificial connotations are evident (Hebrews 9:1–6). Strathmann in Bromiley, *Theological Dictionary*, 503–504.

li. Romans 12:1 uses "therefore" to demonstrate causality in relation to what was addressed in chapter 11, which principally covers the position of Jews and non-Jews in God's providential plan, including the idea that non-Jews were grafted into the tree of Israel. Romans 11 ends with praise to God for such things as the greatness of his knowledge and wisdom.

lii. The renewal of the believer is linked specifically to the work of the Holy Spirit in Titus 3:5, but there it seems to denote a renewal that occurs at the point of salvation, rather than a continual process. Yet, when the various passages cited in our discussion of Romans 12:2 are taken as a whole, it is possible to say that the initial renewal occurs at the point of belief in Jesus' salvific work and that the process of renewal in God's image continues daily through the Holy Spirit.

liii. See also 2 Timothy 4:6 on the use of the same verb related to Paul's life.

liv. According to the Israelite perspective, blood is the life. Notice what Jesus indicated in John 6:53: the only way to have life (eternal) is by consuming his flesh and blood. The comparison to life within human blood appears implicit.

lv. In the next chapter of John, Jesus is remembered for teaching during the Feast of Tabernacles: "If any man is thirsty, let him come to Me and drink. He who believes in Me, as the Scripture said, 'From his innermost being shall flow rivers of living water'" (7:37–38). The subsequent verse explains that the living water is the Holy Spirit. This passage further demonstrates what is found in John 6 that eating and drinking are linked to the idea of belief in Jesus.

lvi. The verb (*ekcheō*), designates the idea of pouring out; Danker, *A Greek-English Lexicon*, 312. When used in reference to pouring out blood, it does have sacrificial implications in the Greek version of the Hebrew Bible (Exodus 29:12), but parts of the Greek version (Deuteronomy 19:10; 21:7) and the New Testament (Matthew 23:29–36) mainly address the spilling of *human* blood in terms of wrongful death.

lvii. On *pascha*, my views align with Danker, *A Greek-English Lexicon*, 784.

lviii. For *airō* and *amnos*, consult Danker, *A Greek-English Lexicon*, 28–29, 54.

lix.　　　While noting that "mercy-seat" is how *hilastērion* has been rendered in English, Danker, *A Greek-English Lexicon*, 474, recommended a translation of "means of expiation" or "place of propitiation."

lx.　　　Matthew and Mark note that the veil was torn just after Jesus died, but Luke does not indicate the exact timing.

Bibliography

Bromiley, Geoffrey W., ed. *Theological Dictionary of the New Testament: Abridged in One Volume.* Grand Rapids: Eerdmans, 1985. Reprint, 1990.

Danker, Frederick W., ed. *A Greek-English Lexicon of the New Testament and other Early Christian Literature.* 3rd ed. Chicago: University of Chicago Press, 2000.

Friberg, Barbara, et al. *Analytical Lexicon of the Greek New Testament.* Grand Rapids: Baker, 2000. BibleWorks electronic edition.

Geyer, John B. "Blood and the Nations in Ritual and Myth." *Vetus Testamentum* 57 (2007) 1–20.

Gilders, William K. *Blood Ritual in the Hebrew Bible: Meaning and Power.* Baltimore: Johns Hopkins University Press, 2004.

Levine, Baruch A. *In the Presence of the Lord: A Study of Cult and Some Cultic Terms in Ancient Israel.* Leiden: Brill, 1974.

Lust, Johan, et al. *Greek-English Lexicon of the Septuagint.* Rev. ed. Stuttgart: Deutsche Bibelgesellschaft, 2003. BibleWorks electronic edition.

Milgrom, Jacob. *Leviticus 1–16.* Anchor Bible 3. Garden City, NY: Doubleday, 1991.

Robertson, Archibald T. *Word Pictures in the New Testament 5.* Nashville: Broadman, 1932.

Szymanski, Terrence. "Reading the Text." http://www.lib.umich.edu/reading/Paul/reading.html/.

Wuest, Kenneth S. *Wuest's Word Studies from the Greek New Testament for the English Reader 2.* Grand Rapids: Eerdmans, 1973. Reprint, 1984.